THE
SECRET LIVES OF
ANIMALS

1,001 Tidbits, Oddities & Amazing Facts about North America's Coolest Animals

Stacy Tornio and Ken Keffer

Illustrations by Rachel Riordan

FALCON GUIDES

GUILFORD, CONNECTICUT
HELENA, MONTANA

To our brothers—Preston, Steve, and Montana.
We loved exploring nature and discovering animals with you growing up.
We hope y'all always stay just a little bit feral.

FALCONGUIDES®

An imprint of Rowman & Littlefield
Falcon, FalconGuides, and Outfit Your Mind are registered trademarks of Rowman & Littlefield.

Distributed by NATIONAL BOOK NETWORK

Copyright © 2016 by Stacy Tornio and Ken Keffer
Illustrations © 2016 by Rachel Riordan

British Library Cataloguing-in-Publication Information available

Library of Congress Cataloging-in-Publication Data available

ISBN 978-1-4930-1191-9 (paperback)
ISBN 978-1-4930-1453-8 (e-book)

♾™ The paper used in this publication meets the minimum requirements of American National Standard for Information Sciences—Permanence of Paper for Printed Library Materials, ANSI/NISO Z39.48-1992.

CONTENTS

ACKNOWLEDGMENTS

This book has been a labor of love. It might be the hardest, yet most rewarding and educational, project we've ever worked on. We want to acknowledge all of our family and friends who have been patient with us as we poured hours of time and research into this book. Thank you so much to Linda Lancaster, Roland Lancaster, Janice Keffer, Rohy Keffer, Steve Tornio, Jack Tornio, Annabelle Tornio, and Scott Schaffer for letting us bounce ideas off of you. (And an extra thanks to our curling team who had to listen to us talk and whine about deadlines during curling season.) Finally, we want to acknowledge some important naturalists and professionals who helped look at content, offer reviews, and give their feedback. Thanks to Kenn Kaufman, Rich Reading, Ben Klasky, and Janice Swainsgood.

FOREWORD

Wild animals! When I was 5 or 6 years old, those two words summed up my interests in life. I talked about animals incessantly, or so I'm told, peppering my parents and my brothers with random amazing facts about this one or that one. No doubt, I was obsessed.

Oddly enough, this interest didn't rise out of my own direct experience. I had been to the zoo only a couple of times. Our suburban neighborhood wasn't wild enough to support even squirrels or chipmunks, let alone the moose or bears or mountain lions that I hoped to see. So after spending yet another afternoon prowling hopefully around the block, I would come home and explore the world of animals through books: library books, gift books from kind relatives. These were my windows to the wilderness.

At some point it crossed my mind that "birds are animals too!" So I decided to take a day or two to figure out the local birdlife. These hitherto-ignored creatures turned out to be fascinating in their own right. And they were so readily available, right outside the door. Who needs gazelles or gorillas when you've got grackles? The more I watched the common birds, the more I was captivated.

Half a century later, I'm still as fascinated as ever. Birds and other animals have given me inspiration, education, adventure, and ultimately a career. I have been fortunate to travel all over the world leading nature tours, teaching courses, writing books and articles, making drawings, taking photos. I've had a chance to meet people from many different cultures and all walks of life, wonderful people who have become treasured friends. This interest in nature has opened doors for learning about everything else.

Of course for most people, a childhood interest in animals won't lead to a career path. But what it can do for everyone is to make life more exciting and more meaningful. The beauty and endless variety of nature can turn every day into a day of discovery. Besides, wild animals go about their lives on their own terms, attuned to the weather and seasons but independent of humans. Paying attention to them helps keep us grounded, connected to the larger world outside ourselves. It's hard to imagine a more wholesome or healthy interest to pursue. If you love a child, one of the best things you can do is to give that child an introduction to the wonders of nature.

I have two good friends who totally understand that—and have been actively doing something about it. Stacy Tornio, an experienced naturalist and gardener, is the recent editor of the tremendously popular *Birds & Blooms* magazine. Communicating about nature comes naturally to her. Ken Keffer has worked as both an educator and a field biologist, doing wildlife research in far-flung places from Wyoming to Mongolia. Certainly these two are well qualified to write about wild animals.

But with all their other qualifications, the most important one is attitude. Whether they're writing, teaching, or just heading outdoors, Stacy and Ken approach nature with excitement and a boundless sense of fun. That's part of the reason I love and admire them so much. The greatest naturalists have retained a childlike sense of wonder, a belief that nature is endlessly amazing. That sense of wonder shines through everything written by Stacy and Ken.

If you want proof, just start reading this book. You'll quickly discover a realm of fun and excitement in the secret lives of animals. For any young person, or anyone who is young at heart, this book is a perfect invitation to the wonderful world of nature.

—Kenn Kaufman, naturalist and author of Kaufman Field Guides

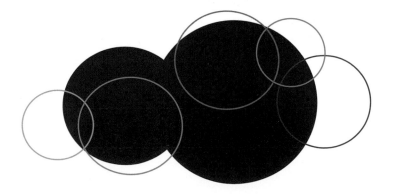

INTRODUCTION

It all started with a harlequin duck. Wait a minute. No—it all started with a killdeer. Okay, okay, it started with a harlequin duck *and* a killdeer. These two birds are our two "spark" birds.

So what is a spark bird? In the birding world, it's very common for people to talk about their spark bird. This usually refers to a specific type of bird or moment that got them excited about birds. Birders all around the world will talk about their spark, and they love sharing it with others.

Ken's spark bird was a harlequin duck. He remembers seeing a picture of it on a sign in his native state of Wyoming. He was completely mesmerized by this duck's bright and beautiful feathers, and he really wanted to see that bird. Even though he'd have to wait many years to see a harlequin duck in person, he still identifies this as an important moment in his life. He even went on to study birds for many years. Actually, he's still studying and learning about birds today.

Stacy's spark bird was a killdeer. This fun bird has a unique habit of pretending to have a broken wing to lure predators away from its nest. During her childhood in Oklahoma, Stacy vividly remembers this bird doing its acting routine, and it's helped give her a lifelong appreciate of all birds. To this day, she loves uncovering their unique habits and antics.

So if people have spark bird moments, don't you think they have spark animal moments too? We definitely think so, and this is pretty much why this book was written.

When it comes to spark moments, or animals in general, it's usually the fun, quirky, and little-known facts that stand out the most. These are the ones that stick with you for a lifetime. And then we had this amazing idea. We thought . . . *What if we wrote an entire book, highlighting the coolest and most unusual facts about animals?*

The idea was an immediate hit. This book features spark-worthy bits about birds, fish, reptiles, and other animals. We pulled together the most fascinating and interesting facts we could find, and we hope you enjoy uncovering them for each animal featured.

Use this book to explore the great outdoors in your area and to uncover the many great animals the natural world has to offer. Hopefully you'll have many of your own spark animals and moments along the way.

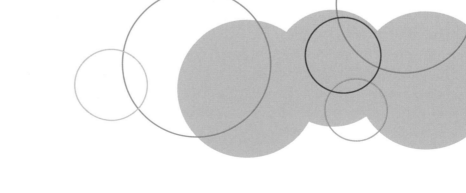

TIPS FOR USING THIS BOOK

There are no wrong ways to read this book. It's a family-friendly book for all ages, and you can enjoy it any way you like. If you want to start reading at the beginning and go straight through to the end, that's totally fine. If you want to flip to page 77 or 107, that's okay too. You can even just go through the table of contents and look for something to catch your eye.

The wonderful illustrations throughout help you figure out what to look for in the wild, and there are some other key icons we want to point out as well. These are standard for each animal we feature:

Types: This tells you the different species of animals.
Size: This gives you an idea of the size of the animal.
Eats: Learn what the featured animal eats.
Eats Them: It's also good to know what eats them!
Range: Discover where you might spot this animal in North America.

We have a few more icons to look for throughout the book. These offer more fun facts, tidbits, and even activities to do.

SCIENCE Q&A: We've featured a few science-based questions and answers throughout the book.

ANIMAL ALL-STAR: The main animals in the book are all from North America, but we wanted to feature some cool world animals through our Animal All-Star picks.

GO OUTSIDE: Like our first book, *The Kids' Outdoor Adventure Book*, we are big advocates of getting outside, so look for this for great ideas.

So there you have it! Go start learning about animals. After all, we have a lot in store. Here's how many animals and facts you can find:

128 ANIMALS

1,001 FACTS

MEET THE LAND INVERTEBRATES

Invertebrates are spineless, but that's not an insult. Literally, invertebrates lack a backbone. This might be about the only thing they all have in common, though. The world of invertebrates that live on land actually includes many unrelated critters. We're talking about everything from insects and worms to spiders and slugs. Let's take a closer look at this large world of animals. (By the way, you can call them "inverts" too!)

Insects are some of the classic invertebrates that we're most familiar with. Insects have three body segments, which you may already know: head, thorax, and abdomen. The antennae, eyes, and mouthparts are attached to the head. Then the six legs and the wings are attached to the thorax. Nearly a million different species of insects have been described by scientists, but nobody really knows how many more have yet to be discovered.

The characteristics described above are all unique to insects. So if you find an invertebrate and it doesn't have six legs, it's not an insect. Maybe it has no legs, like an earthworm. Maybe it has eight legs, like a spider. Perhaps there are so many legs you can't even count them, like a millipede. Just remember that these are all invertebrates, but all invertebrates are not insects.

Of course this makes up a pretty large grouping, which is great if you like to explore and discover new things. Lots of times the best place to look for invertebrates is under something. The next time you're on a hike, try rolling over a log or flipping up a rock. How many invertebrates can you find? Just be sure to return the log or rock carefully to its original place. You don't want to leave your new invertebrate friends homeless.

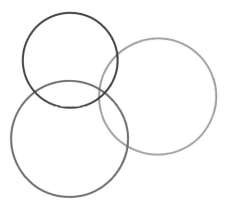

DRAGONFLY

It might be tempting to lump all dragonflies together. After all, they do look similar, zipping up, down, and all around water. But it's worth taking a closer look when you see these fliers because there are many, many species. They seem to come in every color imaginable too. So the next time you see a big-eyed dragonfly flying your way, try to notice its size, color of its body and wings, and more. Then get out an insect book and challenge yourself to identify (ID) it.

LITTLE-KNOWN FACTS

1. Many people think girl dragonflies are called damselflies, but that's not true. Damselflies are just one kind of dragonfly. Damselflies, like the one illustrated, rest with their wings folded behind their bodies, while dragonflies rest with theirs held out to the side.
2. Dragonflies date back more than 300 million years. In fact, fossils show us that they were once quite big. Some records show dragonflies with wingspans of 2 feet. Imagine that flying around!
3. The larval stage of dragonflies can last up to two years. They live underwater, and you might not recognize them as dragonflies.
4. Dragonflies are amazing fliers and hunters. In fact, they combine the two really well, because they do all of their hunting while flying.
5. The lifespan of an adult dragonfly can range from just a couple of weeks to about a year.
6. Dragonflies can eat one hundred or more mosquitoes a day.
7. They have amazing vision. Their two compound eyes can practically see 360 degrees.
8. A few dragonflies, like green darners, will migrate each year.

Types: Thousands of species around the world
Size: Most have a wingspan of 2 to 4 inches and have bodies similar in size.
Eats: Plants, tadpoles, bugs, young fish
Eats Them: Birds, frogs, and other bug-eating animals
Range: Worldwide

GO OUTSIDE

You can find dozens of different dragonfly species right in your own neighborhood. So head outside and challenge yourself to find at least three different-looking dragonflies. You might want to take your binoculars along for a closer look. And get ready, because they sure do move fast! Some of the largest dragonflies can give you a little pinch, so be careful—for their sake as well as yours—if you are handling them.

ANT

Ants can be uninvited guests at a picnic, but they can and do affect the landscape around us. If you want to get a sneak peek of how the underground world of ants operates, you might look into getting a small ant farm that you can keep indoors. Otherwise, be sure to check out the ants outside. Where are they coming from? Where are they going? Are they carrying anything? If you take the time to notice, you can actually learn a lot. Then you'll realize that ants can be really mesmerizing.

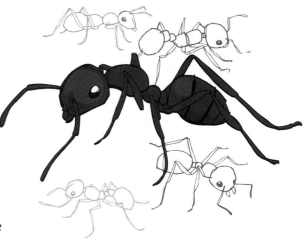

LITTLE-KNOWN FACTS

1. Ants usually live in colonies. Some of these colonies can be extremely large and include more than a million individuals.
2. Most ants are worker ants, while the queen ant lays all the eggs.
3. Male ants have wings, and their main function is to mate with the queen.
4. Communication among ants often involves releasing chemical clues. There's a fancy word for this: "pheromones." Some pheromones help ants know where to go; others can alert the colony of dangers.
5. Most ants can bite or sting. The nonnative fire ants are named for their especially painful bite, which can feel like a little piece of your skin is on fire.

ANIMAL ALL-STAR: Panda Ant

First off, panda ants aren't really ants at all. They are actually in the wasp family, though they don't have wings. Panda ants earned their name because their black-and-white coloring resembles the giant panda. They can give you quite a sting, though, so stay away!

6. Carpenter ants don't make a home in the ground like many other ants. Instead they carve out nest chambers in decomposing wood.

7. Lemon ants, also called citronella ants, give off a citrus scent when their colonies are disturbed.

8. Ants can be found on every continent except ANTarctica.

9. Some species of ants build volcano-shaped hills. Because of the shape, they can be easy to spot. This makes them fun places to observe the comings and goings of an ant colony.

10. E. O. Wilson is a famous scientist and author who has dedicated his career to studying the fascinating ways of ants all over the world.

11. Ants are an important source of food for other critters. They can have a lot of good protein in them. Animals that eat ants can be as small as insects or as large as bears.

12. Ants can carry objects that weigh about fifty times as much as they do! This is pretty amazing for such a little insect.

Types: More than 10,000 species around the world
Size: Less than 1 inch
Eats: Varies by species, but can include seeds, vegetation, other insects, and more
Eats Them: Insects, birds, amphibians, reptiles, mammals (both large and small)
Range: Nearly worldwide

GO OUTSIDE

Watch an ant for an entire 15 minutes. Yes, this is a challenge—you might think you'll get bored after just a couple of minutes. But spend the whole time watching. While watching, write up an ant diary of all the things the ants did. You can even write your own story of the ants' adventures.

WORM

"Worm." What do you think of when you see this word? Maybe you think of a wiggling worm that makes great fishing bait. Or perhaps you think of the worms you uncover while digging in the garden. They might be small and overlooked, but crawlers can be extremely useful. They're pretty darn cute too. Go ahead— try to hold a wiggling worm and not break into a huge grin.

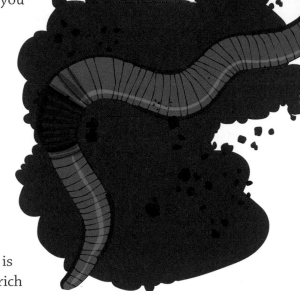

LITTLE-KNOWN FACTS

1. Worm poop, also called castings, is valued by gardeners as nutrient-rich soil. In fact, there's a whole garden movement called vermicomposting that involves planning your garden with worms in mind.
2. Segmented worms are made up of many little segments, so they look like a bunch of rings pushed together. They are also related to leeches and polychaetes.
3. Earthworms have numerous body segments. The head end can sometimes survive if the tail end is damaged, but the tail end won't regenerate. (Flatworms have more regeneration abilities, but they are different altogether.)
4. The longest worms in North America are about a foot long, but some species in other regions can be many feet long.
5. Worms can burrow several feet underground. They like it down there where it's moist and cool.
6. Worms survive the winter by digging some more. They just move down below the frost line.
7. Worms lack lungs, so they use other tactics to breathe. For instance, their mucus helps them transfer oxygen through their skin.

8. Even though they don't have eyes, worms can still detect light from dark.

9. Tiny bristlelike appendages, called setae, help worms crawl along. So imagine these teeny tiny brushes (that you can't even really see) helping them move.

10. Here's a funny word related to worms: clitellum. This is the thick band on earthworms, and it's where they put their eggs.

11. The very popular and well-known night crawlers aren't native to North America. They were introduced here and are quite abundant today.

12. Don't mistake caterpillars for worms. Yes, it's easy to think that all crawlers are a type of worm, but this isn't the case. Caterpillars have a job to do, and that is to turn into beautiful butterflies or moths. Go ahead and try to trick your friends with this one.

Types: Up to 200 species in the United States; many more worldwide
Size: Most species are several inches.
Eats: Vegetation and soil matter
Eats Them: Birds, small mammals, reptiles, amphibians
Range: Widespread throughout the world

GO OUTSIDE

Earthworms are the most popular worms to dig for, but there could be other inverts crawling around in there too. Take your time when you dig, and search for other critters as well. You're like a scientist, searching for the unknown. Just make sure you're not digging in someone's garden!

SCIENCE Q&A: How Do Animals Interact with Each Other?

Animals often interact with other animals, both individuals of the same species and of other species. Sometimes these exchanges can be short and sweet. Other times they are complex. Let's explore some of the different types of relationships between different species of animals.

How about we get the most negative one out of the way first? *Parasitism* happens when one species benefits but the other is harmed from their interactions. Some animals (parasites) depend on other animals for survival. They get all their nutrients from another species (known as the host). The goal of the parasite isn't to kill the host, but sometimes the parasite will make the host weaker or sick. Many parasites are invertebrates. Think of fleas and ticks. They eat the blood of other animals. They aren't like mosquitoes, which dart in and out for a quick meal though. Fleas and ticks can live on the host animal for an extended period.

Mutualism is when both species benefit from their interactions. The cowbirds of North America, like the oxpeckers of Africa, can be examples of mutualism. They'll eat the ticks off large mammals like bison or wildebeest. The mammals benefit because the birds remove parasites from them, and the birds benefit by scoring a meal. Pollination is sometimes thought of as mutualism too. Hummingbirds, bees, and others help pollinate plants while they gain nutrients.

Commensalism can be a little trickier to understand. It is when one species benefits from the relationship, but the other one isn't really affected one way or the other. It doesn't gain a benefit, but it isn't harmed either. If the birds from our earlier example are eating the bugs from the ground that the mammals have stirred up by walking by, that can be considered commensalism. Barnacles living on whales is another example. The barnacles aren't parasites on the whales; they are simply permanent hitchhikers.

Biologists have a fancy term for when things live in close association with each other. It's called *symbiosis*. These interactions can sometimes be positive, but they aren't always. These interactions are what make nature so neat to learn about.

CRICKET

Chirp, chirp, chirp, chirp. Crickets are like the soundtrack of summer. Whenever you hear them on a warm summer night, you can't help but enjoy the season and all it has to offer. They aren't just a good sign in summer, either. In some cultures, crickets can be a sign of good luck. So keep your eyes and ears open. It seems like good things happen when crickets are involved.

LITTLE-KNOWN FACTS

1. Crickets' ears are on their legs.
2. Females have a long thin thing behind their body called an ovipositor. It looks like a tail or a stinger, but it is harmless and used to deposit eggs.
3. Want to know how crickets make their signature sound? They do it by rubbing special parts of their wings together.
4. Like their relatives, the grasshoppers and katydids, crickets go through a simple metamorphosis, or transformation. After they hatch from an egg, crickets look like miniature adults. They can molt (shed a smaller body for a bigger one) several times to grow bigger. So if you find two crickets, compare their sizes. Maybe you'll have both a younger and older cricket.
5. Crickets chirp louder and faster as the temperature raises. Some people think you can use this to figure out the temperature, but this is a myth. You can only get a rough estimate at best.
6. Despite looking similar, mole crickets, camel crickets, and Jerusalem crickets aren't related to one another or to true crickets.
7. Crickets are also raised on farms for animal food. They are even becoming more popular as human food, so look for cricket flour on your grocery store shelf in the coming years.
8. The antennae on crickets are called feelers. They allow the crickets to feel their way around at night, when they are most active.

Types: Over 120 species in North America; many more around the world
Size: Most are 1 inch or less.
Eats: Vegetation, some insects
Eats Them: All insect eaters, including frogs and birds
Range: Worldwide

MANTID

Mantids are masters of camouflage, and you'll have to look close to spot one. They have an amazing ability to blend into their surroundings. If you can't find a mantid, try searching for their egg casings in late summer. These brown, ball-like structures are usually attached to stems, and they're fascinating. Don't be tempted to take them inside, though. If you do, you'll have hundreds of miniature mantids scurrying about when they hatch. Yes, there really are that many eggs in the casings!

LITTLE-KNOWN FACTS

1. Is it praying mantis or praying mantid? You can almost use the words interchangeably, though you'll sound more like a scientist if you know the difference. *Mantis* is in the mantid group. So all members of the *Mantis* genus are mantids, but not all mantids are *Mantis*.
2. Praying mantids get their name because when they put their front legs together, it looks like they are praying.
3. Look closely at the praying mantid's head. It is in the shape of a triangle.
4. There are tropical praying mantids called flower mantids. They are found in warmer areas and often have bright colors like reds and greens.
5. Female mantids are often larger than males. However, they have smaller wings in many cases. Try to gather up a couple of mantids and compare.
6. Praying mantids have been known to stalk and kill hummingbirds. Look for mantids that might lurk around hummingbird feeders, waiting to attack.
7. Even though they look nothing alike, these insects are closely related to termites and cockroaches.

Types: More than 1,000 mantid species around the world
Size: Up to 6 inches
Eats: Other insects, plants
Eats Them: Frogs, reptiles, birds, other small animals
Range: Worldwide, plus they really like warm areas

ANIMAL ALL-STAR: Devil's Flower Mantis

Mantids are already pretty fascinating creatures, but the devil's flower mantis takes it to a whole new level. This praying mantis can mimic the look of a plant called devil's flower, which is a kind of orchid. It will sit there as still as can be, and then when something comes along—unsuspecting of anything—it will attack!

CICADA

The scientific name for cicada roughly means "tree cricket," but these aren't real crickets. They aren't related to locusts either, even though many people apply this term to them. Cicadas are big-bodied insects with large wings. And they sure are noisy! You know summer has arrived when you hear the echo of cicadas throughout the woods.

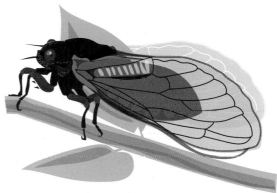

LITTLE-KNOWN FACTS

1. Some species fall under the label of annual cicadas because the adults are present every single year. Others are known as periodic cicadas, since adults only emerge every few years.
2. If you think it's interesting that some cicadas only come out every few years, then you'll really be impressed to know that some adult cicadas have much longer cycles. For example, some species can emerge up to seventeen years apart!
3. Cicadas can be pale when they first emerge from their nymph stage. After a short time, they get a lot darker.

4. Cicadas rid themselves of excess fluids they don't need. It is kind of like cicada pee, but some people call it honey dew. The next time you think you feel a "raindrop" under a tree, you might want to think again.
5. Cicada killers have earned their name. They are a group of wasps that specialize in eating cicadas.
6. Where does the cicada sound come from? It comes from a special membrane, and the sound is then loudly broadcast through the abdomen. Yep, that's right. They make music through their tummies!

Types: Approximately 3,000 species
Size: Usually 1–2 inches
Eats: Plant material, sap
Eats Them: Birds, small mammals, fish
Range: Worldwide

GO OUTSIDE

Look for cicada casings left behind. You'll often see the brown shells on trees or other plants. They might make you do a double take—they can look exactly like a cicada.

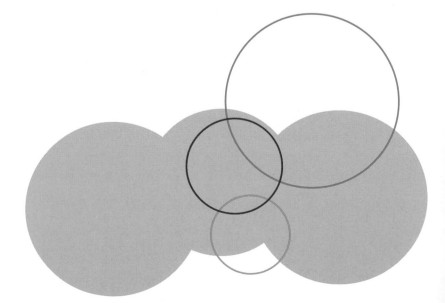

BEETLE

Beetles are abundant and diverse. They are the most numerous type of critter around, and there could be as many as 25,000 different species of beetle in the United States alone. The term "could be" is an important thing to note. Because there are so many, scientists are sure there are more species that haven't even been discovered. The ones that have been discovered are as unique and different as ladybugs, weevils, dung beetles, Hercules beetles, and longhorn beetles. There are even aquatic beetle species. With all these species to choose from, how can you possibly pick a favorite?

LITTLE-KNOWN FACTS

1. Most beetles have specially modified forewings called elytra, which form a hard, protective outer shell.
2. Beetles use their hind wings for flight.
3. Beetles use their strong mandibles to chew, which is a pretty rare characteristic for insects.
4. There are estimates of more than 350,000 known beetle species, but some researchers estimate there could be as many as 3 million species total. This means there's a lot left to discover!
5. A single ladybug beetle can eat more than 2,500 aphids in its lifetime.
6. Many species of beetles use chemical repellents to keep them safe from potential predators. Two extreme examples of this are the bombardier and blister beetles, which can cause a lot of pain to human skin.
7. Beetles have been around for more than 230 million years.
8. You might say that beetles are big fans of poop. Some species of dung beetle eat poop. Others lay their eggs in it.
9. Mealworms, which are popular for feeding to birds, are the larval stage of a beetle.

10. Some species of beetles are considered pests because of the damage they do to crops and trees. Many of these are not native to North America and have been introduced (often accidentally) from other areas.

Types: More than 25,000 species in the United States
Size: Most are less than 1 inch, though some can be larger.
Eats: Most eat plant materials; some eat insects, meat, or fungi.
Eats Them: Birds, small mammals, insects, fish
Range: Worldwide

GO OUTSIDE

Count the spots on a ladybug. Some people say this helps tell their age, but this isn't actually true. However, it can help you find out what type of ladybug you're looking at. For instance, one with seven spots is likely the seven-spotted ladybug. So count those spots, find a good field guide or ID book, and see what you can find out.

FIREFLY

Of all the species of beetles out there, fireflies are some of the most celebrated, so they deserve their own entry. (Yes, fireflies are a type of beetle.) These little fliers, best known as lightning bugs for giving off a soft glow on warm summer nights, bring lots of fun to backyards across the country. The next time you go out looking for fireflies at dusk, keep some of the following odd and interesting facts in mind. Then share them with your friends to teach them a thing or two.

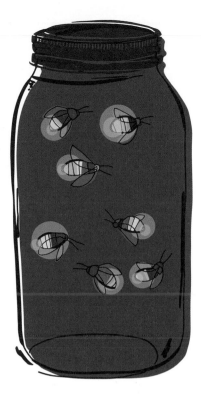

LITTLE-KNOWN FACTS

1. Not all firefly species have the ability to glow. But this fancy glow also has a fancy name. It is called bioluminescence.
2. The light that fireflies give off is their way of communicating with one another. Often this glow is used to attract another firefly.
3. Fireflies will eat one another. In fact, some fireflies will glow just to lure in another one. Then they will eat it. Now that's really a sneak attack!

ANIMAL ALL-STAR: Fairyfly

Do you know what the tiniest insect in the world is? It's the fairyfly. These little fliers are part of the wasp family, and you can find them in warm areas. Humans barely even notice them, though, because of their tiny size. They can be as little as about 0.0055 inch long. That's not quite as big as the period at the end of this sentence.

4. You can help scientists learn more about fireflies by signing up online for the firefly watch. This is a cool way to get involved in citizen science. Sign up through the Museum of Science at mos.org.

5. While fireflies do exist in most parts of the world, it's hard to find them in parts of the West. Coauthor Ken Keffer did not grow up with fireflies in Wyoming, but coauthor Stacy Tornio did grow up with them in Oklahoma.

Types: More than 2,000 species
Size: Around an inch or less
Eats: Pollen, plants, other insects
Eats Them: Many bug-eating predators, such as birds, frogs, lizards
Range: Worldwide in warm environments

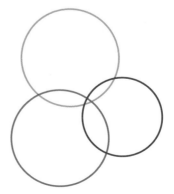

GO OUTSIDE

If you've never spent an evening catching fireflies, then now is the time. The classic method is to get a clear jar and punch holes in the top. You can also take a mesh bag (like a laundry bag) and turn it upside down as a way of capturing them. Try to collect ten to twelve, and then watch how they light up your container. Do you notice their different flashing patterns? Be sure to release them after a short while.

SCORPION

Many venomous critters get a bad rap, and scorpions are no exception. Even the name sounds a bit menacing, doesn't it? Scorpions are nocturnal creatures for the most part, meaning they move around at night. People in the Southwest know to watch out for scorpions. In fact, they'll often check their shoes in case any scorpions came along to find a place to rest during the night. While most species aren't dangerous to people, getting stung by a scorpion wouldn't be fun. This is one insect where you should err on the side of safety.

LITTLE-KNOWN FACTS

1. When there's not a lot of food around, scorpions can slow their metabolism to conserve their energy, which helps them survive better. No wonder they're so resilient.
2. While scorpions are tough survivors, there is one thing they really can't live without. Scorpions need soil because they'll burrow down into it.
3. Scientists can't exactly explain why, but if you put scorpions under an ultraviolet light, they look fluorescent. What a cool trick!
4. Scorpions can have as many as six to twelve eyes, but their eyesight is pretty poor overall. Their poor eyesight and overall sensitivity to light are major reasons they mostly come out at night.
5. When they are really little, young scorpions will often ride on their mother's backs.
6. Antarctica is the only place you won't find scorpions living.

7. Even though most scorpions won't harm you, there is one species in the United States that could potentially kill a person. It's the Arizona bark scorpion. Especially if that person is sensitive to the venom. This is one of the reasons you should definitely take them seriously!

Types: 1,500 species around the world
Size: Just a few inches to more than 8 inches
Eats: Insects, spiders, lizards, other scorpions
Eats Them: Rodents, snakes, lizards
Range: Found worldwide

ANIMAL ALL-STAR: Giant Prickly Stick

This insect looks like a cross between a stick and a cactus. One of its defense mechanisms is that it will curl up its body to mimic a scorpion. Of course they can't do a lot of harm, but predators don't know this. Here's the most fun fact of all about this crawler—it smells like peanut butter to humans!

BUTTERFLY

It seems like everyone loves butterflies, and rightfully so. They are amazing and beautiful, often sporting bright colors and patterns. The monarch butterfly is perhaps the most recognized and popular butterfly, but there are many more species in the United States. You should learn about butterflies beyond the monarch, because they truly are fascinating creatures. Some people like to keep track of all the different species they've ever seen. They call it a life list, and it's similar to the way people keep track of the number of birds they see. How many species can you say you've seen? Time to get out the butterfly book!

LITTLE-KNOWN FACTS

1. Many people say that butterflies emerge from cocoons, but this is not true. Moths come from cocoons. Butterflies emerge from the same type of thing, but it's called a chrysalises. Go ahead and trick your friends with this one!

2. Butterflies use their feet to taste with. Now that is being resourceful.

3. Butterflies have a really cool tongue. It's called a proboscis. It stays curled up, and then they uncurl it and use it like a straw to sip up nectar.

4. Yes, butterflies eat nectar, but that's not all. They'll engage in an activity called puddling. It's where they gather at mud puddles and soak up nutrients from the mud and other materials (sometimes even pee and poop).

5. Butterflies absolutely love hot weather. In fact, if it's cold they're often not able to fly. Their body temperature has to be 86°F in order to fly. You know how you wake up early with the birds? Well, then you stay up for the butterflies, because they are most active by midmorning.

6. The largest butterfly is the Queen Alexandra birdwing butterfly, with a wingspan of a foot wide. It lives in New Guinea, and it's worth noting that the female is bigger than the male.

7. Monarchs migrate for winter, but this is a unique behavior for butterflies. When they travel south, they gather up in large groups in late summer

ANIMAL ALL-STAR:
Glasswing Butterfly

This is one cool butterfly because of its amazing see-through wings! You won't find this butterfly in much of the United States except maybe Florida, where it will go at times. It's much more common in southern parts of Mexico and through Columbia. This is definitely a butterfly you have to see in person. It's so cool!

and fall. Then they roost by the thousands at night. This is quite a phenomenon if you ever get the chance to see it.

8. Here's a good trick for telling the difference between a male and female monarch: Males have a little added dot along the lower part of their wings. You can see this on both sides, especially when they have their wings out. Females lack this little spot.

9. Most butterfly adults only live for two to four weeks total.

10. Many butterflies are brightly colored as a defense mechanism. Bright colors are often a warning sign in the wild, so this helps deter predators.

11. Many butterflies have host plants, so they lay their eggs on a specific type of plant. Monarchs only lay their eggs on milkweed. It's important to plant host plants in your backyard to support all butterfly populations.

12. After butterflies lay their eggs, little caterpillars (also called larvae) hatch. They are caterpillars before they create a chrysalis. If you find a caterpillar in your area, take a picture and try to figure out what kind of butterfly or moth it eventually will be.

Types: 700-plus species in the United States alone
Size: Several species can be less than an inch, though monarchs and swallow-tails are several inches.

Eats: Nectar, plants while they are caterpillars
Eats Them: Many insect-eaters, including frogs, birds, lizards
Range: Tons of butterfly species in every part of the world

GO OUTSIDE

Every summer there are events held to count butterflies. This helps scientists learn about the butterfly populations and how they are doing. Get involved in a counting event near you—or just count on your own. You can learn more through the North American Butterfly Association website: naba.org.

MOTH

Moths are sometimes the overlooked cousins of butterflies. Moths and butterflies look similar at first glance, but there are some key differences. No, it's not that butterflies are bright and moths are not, because in reality there are brown butterflies and also brightly colored moths. After you learn these cool facts, you're going to want to be on the lookout for moths just as much as you are for butterflies. Don't worry—there are easy ways to attract them. For starters, you can try to attract them by leaving your porch light on at night.

LITTLE-KNOWN FACTS

1. One of the biggest differences between moths and butterflies is that moths have straight or feathery antennae, while butterflies' antennae have a knob at the end.

2. While most people think of moths as being night fliers (yes, many truly are), this isn't always the case. Sphinx moths are active during the day.

3. Here's another trick to telling the difference between moths and butterflies. Most moths hold their wings flat against their body (or straight out) when they rest, while butterflies generally hold their wings out behind them.

4. Many moths don't eat at all. Some don't even have mouthparts.

5. Most adult moths only live for a week or two.

6. People in other countries eat caterpillars regularly, including moth caterpillars. This is because they provide good nutrition.

7. The largest moth in the world is the Atlas moth of Taiwan, with a wingspan of more than a foot.

8. Moths are so popular that they actually have a week designated in their name. Look for National Moth Week, which takes place every year in July.

Types: More than 10,000 species in the United States alone
Size: Mostly range from less than ½ inch to several inches
Eats: Nectar, plants, sometimes nothing at all
Eats Them: Birds, frogs, spiders, other animals that eat insects
Range: Thousands of species in all parts of the world

GO OUTSIDE

Want to attract moths? Besides leaving your porch light on, you can also use a special bait to attract them. Make a paste of mashed banana and brown sugar or molasses, then just smear it on a tree and wait for them to come. Black lights can also be used to attract night fliers.

CENTIPEDE

Lots of people lump centipedes and millipedes together, but they aren't related. Not even close. People think of them together, but they never take time to count their legs. Centipedes only have one pair of legs per segment. A lot of invertebrates are decomposers (so they break down dead or decaying matter), but not centipedes. They are agile predators making meals out of insects and other invertebrates. Some can pinch or bite surprisingly hard, so it is best to observe with your eyes and not your hands.

LITTLE-KNOWN FACTS

1. If you can't count the legs, you can still identify a centipede because centipede bodies go from side to side like an "S" when they move.
2. It's a common myth that centipedes have one hundred legs. This is not true; actually, the number of legs can vary a great deal. Some centipedes might have 30, while others have more than 300. Also, millipedes don't have 1,000 legs like some people say. Most have fewer than 100.
3. If a centipede loses a leg, it can grow (regenerate) a new one.
4. House centipedes have extra-long legs and are often found inside homes. They are harmless to people, though.
5. The largest centipede in the world is the tiger centipede of South America. It can grow up to 12 inches, and it is striped like a tiger.

Types: More than 8,000 centipedes species
Size: Smaller than an inch to several inches
Eats: Mostly other invertebrates
Eats Them: Reptiles, amphibians, birds, some mammals
Range: Every part of the world

MILLIPEDE

They might look alike at first glance, but what makes centipedes and millipedes different? Millipedes have two pairs of legs on each body segment. If you can't count the legs, you can still identify a millipede because millipede bodies stay straight when they move.

LITTLE-KNOWN FACTS

1. When a millipede feels threatened, it will curl up into a little circle for protection.
2. It can also release a foul-tasting and -smelling chemical as a defense.
3. There are more than 1,400 species of millipede in the United States and Canada, and it can be difficult to tell them all apart.
4. Fossils show that millipedes were some of the earliest critters to breathe air and live on land.
5. Both centipedes and millipedes can live for a surprisingly long time—up to three to five years in many cases.

Types: More than 12,000 species
Size: Smaller than an inch to several inches
Eats: Mostly plants and decaying matter
Eats Them: Reptiles, amphibians, birds, some mammals
Range: Every part of the world

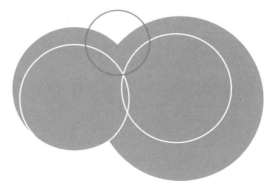

SPIDER

Don't you dare call a spider an insect! The often-feared but ever-so-cool spiders are classified as arachnids. It's their eight legs that give them away as not being insects (since most insects have a mere six legs). Most people associate spiders with webs. And while it's true that they are known for making webs to catch food, this isn't true for all spiders. So what else is different about the arachnids that you thought you knew? Here are some more fascinating facts.

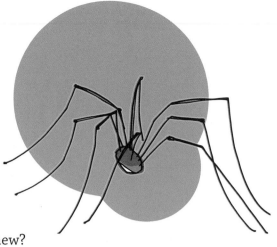

LITTLE-KNOWN FACTS

1. The thing that makes spiders different from other arachnids (like scorpions) is their ability to produce silk. While silk is used to make webs, spiders also use it for other purposes, like lowering themselves through the air or protecting their eggs.
2. Spiders share another habit with scorpions. They inject venom into their prey to kill them. All spiders except one family use venom.

ANIMAL ALL-STAR: Goliath Birdeater Tarantula

This tarantula is among the largest in its family, and it's common in South America. A lot of times tarantulas like this one get a bad reputation because they are big and hairy, and some people think they are scary. The thing is, most of them can't do any damage to humans at all! In fact, they are really starting to gain popularity as pets.

3. Even though most spiders have eight eyes, most spiders can't see very well with them. Some spider species (like the cave-dwelling spiders) don't even have eyes at all.
4. Tarantulas are well-known spiders, and yes, they do exist in North America—mostly in southwest areas. Most of the tarantulas in North America are brown or black, but those in other parts of the world can have bright colors.
5. The classic spider web—rounded and getting smaller as you move more into the center—is usually woven by orb weaver spiders.
6. Not all spiders have webs. For instance, wolf spiders don't spin webs. Jumping spiders don't, either. They just jump on their prey.
7. Some female spiders can lay a few hundred eggs at a time.
8. While spiders are venomous, most are pretty harmless. Plus they eat many bugs, so go ahead and support most spider populations. They aren't anything to shriek over.
9. Some reports say that as many as 50 percent of people are afraid of spiders. This fear is called arachnophobia.

Types: More than 40,000 species around the world
Size: They can be a few inches, but most are less than an inch.
Eats: Small insects like flies
Eats Them: Birds, wasps, reptiles
Range: Many types of spiders throughout the world

GO OUTSIDE

Grab your magnifying glass and head outside to look for a spider web. Once you find one, use your magnifying glass to carefully study the web pattern. Notice how it's woven very close together, which will help them trap their prey. Be careful, and make sure you don't break the web.

BEE

Next time you see a bee buzzing about, be sure to thank it. Much of the food you eat is a direct result of bees. How is that possible? Here's why: Pollination is essential for plants to develop, grow, and produce. This makes bees essential to people. Having bees around ensures we have food. The bee populations have been declining over the past several years, so it's important to do what you can to help them thrive and survive.

LITTLE-KNOWN FACTS

1. Bee colonies or hives are led by female leaders, called queen bees.
2. Bees have two compound eyes. This means they are made up of thousands of tiny lenses. They also have three more eyes on top of the compound ones.
3. In a single lifetime, a honeybee produces about one-tenth of a teaspoon of honey. Imagine how many bees and how much work it takes to produce a single jar.
4. Queen bees can lay 1,000 eggs a day and more than 1 million in a lifetime!
5. Bees in a hive all have different jobs. Some worker bees make the honeycomb, while others go out to gather the nectar and pollen. When they have a job, they usually have it for life.
6. In a bee colony, the queen and all the worker bees are females. Male bees (called drones) are only around in spring, but then it's the girls that do all the work.
7. Worker bees might only live three or four weeks before the next generation comes along to work in the hive. The queen bee lives three or four years.
8. Only certain species of bees make honey. Many more bee species aren't honey-makers at all.
9. At its peak, a bee colony could contain as many as 40,000 to 60,000 bees.

10. Here's an exhausting fact: Bees don't really sleep. They are active 24 hours a day, always working.

Types: More than 1,000 honeybees and related species worldwide
Size: Around ⅛ inch to 1 inch
Eats: Nectar and pollen from flowers
Eats Them: Some birds; animals like foxes and skunks will attack beehives.
Range: Worldwide

GO OUTSIDE

Many people are afraid of bees, but there's no reason to be in most cases. (Of course, if you're allergic to bee stings, you definitely have a reason.) In fact, the bee population needs our help to survive. During spring or summer, plant some flowers just for the bees. You can research good flowers for bees (bee balm is a good one) or ask someone at the garden center for a recommendation.

ANIMAL ALL-STAR:
Madagascar Hissing Cockroach

This is one of the biggest cockroaches around, and it'll get to be about 2 or 3 inches. If you were to find old or rotting wood in Madagascar, there's a good chance you would come across this crawler. You've probably guessed it by now, but yes, these cockroaches do give off a hissing sound. It's important to note that this hissing sound isn't actually a vocalization. It's the sound of air going through tiny holes on their backs.

WASP

Wasps are intriguing creatures, and they are a lot more diverse than you might think. Some wasps might buzz your juice when you're taking a snack break outside. Others tend to mind their own business. Some live in large colonies, building their own paper-like nests out of wood pulp or mud, while others live in solitude. Some wasps are pollinators and provide benefits similar to bees. Other species are efficient predators of other invertebrates. If a wasp is invading your space, don't panic. It might check you out but will mostly likely leave you alone.

LITTLE-KNOWN FACTS

1. Velvet ants are actually a type of wingless wasps. These velvety "ants" are really the females.
2. Digger wasps have unique hunting habits. The female catches an insect, paralyzes it, and then buries it in the nest.
3. While most people dislike and even kill wasps, these insects actually do more good than harm. They really can help take care of other insect populations, so try letting them be.
4. Some wasps build amazing, intricate nests that look like papery material.
5. Social wasps often stay together in groups. Two common types include yellow jackets and paper wasps.
6. Wasps die every year except for the new or younger queens. They will hibernate for winter and come out in spring to form a new colony.
7. Wasps have a short life. They generally live only ten to twenty days.

Types: More than 10,000 species worldwide
Size: Most less than an inch, though some can reach 1½ inches.
Eats: Caterpillars and other small insects
Eats Them: Frogs, toads, lizards, spiders
Range: Worldwide

SCIENCE Q&A: Do People Eat Invertebrates?

Have you ever been riding your bike when suddenly a bug hits you right in the face? Maybe you swallowed it down before you even realized what happened. Have you ever wondered if people eat insects on purpose?

Sure, lots of people really enjoy eating invertebrates, like shrimp, crab, lobster, and oysters. But what about insects? The answer is yes. In many parts of the world insects are a regular part of the diet. Nearly 2,000 invertebrate species have been consumed around the globe. Beetles, mealworms, caterpillars, scorpions, spiders, grasshoppers, cicadas, and crickets are some of the most widespread.

Insects as food are growing in popularity in the United States too. And not just joke foods like chocolate-covered grasshoppers, either. One of the easiest ways to incorporate insects into the human diet is in the form of cricket flour. Cricket flour is nutrient packed, easy to use, and—perhaps the best part—you don't have any eyes or legs to get caught between your teeth.

Some people like to snack on ants too. They can have a refreshing burst of citrus lemon flavor. Be careful if you try this yourself, though. They tend to bite you before you can bite them. Fire ants should probably be avoided.

Insects can be easily raised, and they don't require much food, water, or space. Many are responsible for pollinating the food we eat. But others can also be the food we eat. Don't expect them to completely take over the menu though. Hamburgers and chicken nuggets are probably here to stay.

TICK

Ticks will probably find you before you find them, which gives lots of people the heebie-jeebies. Yes, it's not really a pleasant thought to think of ticks "finding" you. They might also look for your dog to climb on for their next meal. They are truly the ultimate sit-and-wait critter. They just hang out waiting for an animal to pass by. Then they climb on and settle in for their next home.

LITTLE-KNOWN FACTS

1. Ticks rely on blood for survival. They will travel from one animal to the next to feed. This pretty much sums up their entire lives.
2. Ticks have soft stomachs that allow them to expand (like little balloons) as they consume blood.
3. Ticks occasionally carry diseases that can affect pets and humans. Lyme disease is one of the most common, so you should remove ticks as soon as possible when you find them.
4. Ticks are a type of arachnid, which means they are related to spiders. Go ahead and do the leg test. Sure enough, they have eight legs to prove it.
5. There's a myth floating around that ticks fall on you from above. Actually ticks are crawlers and often crawl up legs.

Types: More than 600 species worldwide
Size: Around 1⁄16 inch to 3⁄8 inch
Eats: Blood
Eats Them: Anything that eats small insects
Range: Worldwide

GRASSHOPPER

Take a summer walk in the prairie, and the grasshoppers will likely scatter like popping popcorn in all directions. You can hardly watch where one lands before another one takes off and distracts you. Grasshopper watching (and catching) is a great activity for any age. Sneaking up on a grasshopper and trying to catch it is an entertaining, and often challenging, way to spend an afternoon.

LITTLE-KNOWN FACTS

1. Females grasshoppers are larger than the males in most cases.
2. Unlike crickets (closely related), which use their wings to make sound, grasshoppers make sound by rubbing their legs or other body parts together.
3. Do you know where grasshoppers have their ears? They're on their bellies!
4. Most people think of grasshoppers as being great hoppers, and they are. But they have wings and can fly, as well.

ANIMAL ALL-STAR: Weta

This massive insect looks like a giant grasshopper. Even its great name translates to "fierce grasshopper." The giant weta is native to New Zealand, and it's one of the heaviest insects in the world. It can weigh as much as three AA batteries. This might not seem like a lot at first, but remember, this is an insect!

5. Locusts and grasshoppers are the same thing in many cases. Here's an easy way to remember it: All locusts are grasshoppers, but not all grasshoppers are locusts.
6. When grasshoppers get together, they can do a lot of harm. Called locusts, large grasshopper groups can destroy farm crops.
7. Have you ever had a grasshopper "spit" at you? They produce this brown liquid material, which is a type of self-defense. It might seem like they are spitting at you, but it won't hurt you at all.
8. Some species of lubber grasshoppers have stubby wings and are not able to fly.

Types: 10,000 species around the world
Size: Range from ⅜ inch to more than 3 inches
Eats: Plant material
Eats Them: Frogs, birds, reptiles, other bug-eaters
Range: Worldwide

GO OUTSIDE

Gather up some family or friends and try out the grasshopper challenge. The rules are simple: Just set a time limit (like 15 or 30 minutes), and see how many grasshoppers you can catch during that time. You can divide into teams or have everyone be on his or her own.

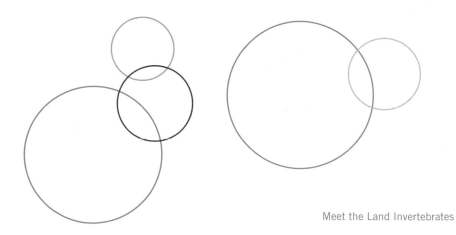

FLEA

If you have a pet, you're likely going to meet a flea at some point. These little critters are pretty tiny, so you don't always see them easily. But if you have them in your area, they are hard to miss. This is because these parasites feed on blood and cause major itching. So if you're itching or you notice your pets scratching, it's probably time to take a closer look.

LITTLE-KNOWN FACTS

1. Fleas need animals to survive. They are attracted by body heat, and they live on animals like dogs, rabbits, rodents, cats, and even people.
2. Young fleas stay in their cocoons until they sense an animal nearby. Then they emerge and jump onboard.
3. Fleas can often be high carriers of disease. If your animal has fleas, it's best to get rid of them right away.
4. Here's another animal where the female lays lots of eggs. She can lay up to 2,000 in her lifetime.
5. Many fleas can jump up to 8 inches. This is a pretty huge feat, considering they are so tiny.

Types: More than 200 species of fleas worldwide
Size: Most are only about 1/20 inch.
Eats: Blood
Eats Them: Spiders, ants, other insect-eaters
Range: Worldwide

FLY

Flies don't have the best reputation. They are usually an insect you want to swat away, so you're not going to encourage or welcome them. Who can blame you? You'll often see flies buzzing around food or around animals outside on a hot day, and you don't want them landing on your food. Before you swat them, discover a few cool facts. With thousands upon thousands of species worldwide, some of these facts have to be new to you.

LITTLE-KNOWN FACTS

1. Mosquitoes are actually a type of fly. There are some 3,000 species of mosquitoes worldwide, but they are definitely part of the fly family.
2. There are many other "flies," including dragonflies and fireflies, that aren't actually flies at all.
3. For mosquitoes and many other types of flies, the females are the ones that do the biting.
4. The next time you see a bee, you might want to take a closer look. (Remember, if you leave them alone, they'll usually leave you alone.) There's a whole family of flies called bee flies that look a lot like bees—it's a defense mechanism.
5. You've heard of maggots, right? They look like little pieces of wiggling rice. Well maggots are just young flies in their larval stage.
6. A typical housefly can move its wings up to 200 times per second.
7. Houseflies generally live only a month or so.
8. Houseflies can survive so well because they can lay thousands of eggs in their short lifetime. So even if most of those eggs don't make it, houseflies are still reproducing at high rates.

Types: More than 150,000 species around the world
Size: Most are very small, but some of the largest include horseflies, which get to be more than an inch.
Eats: Fungi, plants, fruit, poop
Eats Them: Frogs, birds, other small animals
Range: You'll find hundreds of fly species just about anywhere you go.

SNAIL

Wouldn't it be handy to just haul your home around with you everywhere you went? This is what a snail does. It hauls around a shell, which it also relies on for protection. You can find snails in just about any damp area in the world. They will burrow in the mud if it gets too hot, and they'll hibernate in winter.

LITTLE-KNOWN FACTS

1. Most snails in North America are only a few inches long, but the giant African land snail can be more than a foot long.
2. Snails can't hear, but they can see.
3. Fossil snails have been found from over 600 million years ago.
4. You can't tell the difference between male and female snails because they are both. This is called a hermaphrodite.
5. Snails have what is called a radula. This is a tongue covered with lots of sharp little "teeth."
6. Some of the most common snails in the United States are the garden snails. Look for them in your garden.

Types: Thousands of species
Size: Most are just a few inches.
Eats: Algae, limestone, sometimes each other
Eats Them: Birds, frogs, other small animals
Range: In damp areas worldwide

GO OUTSIDE

Here's something you can do with snails or slugs: Find snail or slug "slime," which they leave behind when they move, and take a closer look at it. Don't worry, it's not going to hurt you. Some people even think it can be used as a medicine for certain things. If you don't want to touch it, at least get a closer look at it.

SLUG

Slugs have a reputation for being slimy, kind of gross, and a nuisance in the garden. It's true that these crawlers can cause damage to plants, but try to overlook that for a minute and take a look at what makes them so interesting. Some of these facts might explain why there are so many of them too.

LITTLE-KNOWN FACTS

1. Slugs can lay 400 to 500 eggs in a single year.
2. In a single lifetime, slugs can go through thousands of "teeth." This is because when one set of teeth starts to wear out, a new set comes through to replace them.
3. The slimy trail that slugs leave behind them as they go is in large part a defense mechanism—this fluid tastes bad to predators.
4. Scientists estimate that at any given time, only 5 percent of the slug population is out and about. So if you're trying to get rid of slugs, just know that there are many more. Most are probably underground.
5. It would likely take a slug a couple of hours to move just 100 yards.
6. An old method of slug control is to pour salt on it. While this does work by drying them out, it's a pretty slow and awful way to die. Use a different method for controlling slugs instead, like the product Sluggo. Or you can just let them be.
7. The banana slug found in the United States can get more than a foot long.

Types: Thousands of species in the world, but a few dozen in the United States
Size: Most are a few inches.
Eats: Lots of plants, especially in the backyard garden
Eats Them: Birds, frogs, reptiles, other small animals
Range: Worldwide

MEET THE WATER INVERTEBRATES

Just like the land inverts, water invertebrates don't have backbones, but other than that, they have very little in common. This is because in most cases they aren't related to each other at all. Many, but not all, are arthropods, which are related to insects, spiders, and even crabs. Arthropods share characteristics—for instance, they all have an exoskeleton, segmented bodies, and jointed legs.

Some of the most common aquatic invertebrates include crabs and their relatives, lobsters, crayfish, shrimp, krill, and barnacles. Collectively, these are known as crustaceans. Some can be found in freshwater, but many are more abundant in the oceans.

While there are some very large invertebrates, most are pretty small. This doesn't mean they aren't important, though! Lots of critters like to eat invertebrates, for example. Invertebrates can eat lots too, which is good for everyone overall. This is because many are decomposers and eat dead plants or animals; without invertebrates, nutrients wouldn't be cycled as easily.

Since they live in the water, aquatic invertebrates can sometimes be hard to see. You can use tools to help you find aquatic invertebrates. For instance, you can try a bucket or a net to scoop them up for a closer look. No matter what tools you use, get out there and explore water invertebrates. They are often overlooked, but they're definitely worth taking the time to notice.

JELLYFISH

Jellyfish can vary quite a bit in behavior from one species to the next. Some move around a lot, while others do not. Some are strong hunters; others mostly wait for the food to come to them. No matter what, these squishy-bodied sea creatures are pretty cool. Many people think they are dangerous, but it's time to get the facts straight.

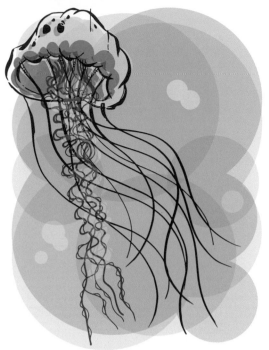

LITTLE-KNOWN FACTS

1. Jellyfish aren't fish.
2. Jellyfish do not have a brain.
3. Jellyfish that sting (not all do) have tentacles that contain venom. This is how they catch their prey, because they capture and shock them.
4. Where is a jellyfish's mouth? It's not where you might think it is. It's really hard to see because it's directly under its dome-shaped body.
5. You can actually help scientists monitor jellyfish. Whether you live near jellyfish areas or you're just visiting, help out with this citizen science project by observing the jellyfish in the area. Then go and record your sightings at jellywatch.org.
6. When jellyfish gather in large groups (sometimes there will be thousands), it's called a bloom. Jellyfish blooms are very cool phenomena.

Types: More than 200 species
Size: Bodies of a few inches to several feet
Eats: Eggs, smaller fish, larvae
Eats Them: Sea turtles, some fish
Range: A variety of species worldwide

SCIENCE Q&A:
What Is the Intertidal Zone?

The intertidal zone is a unique place. It can be home to lots of cool aquatic invertebrates, among other things. But before we get into the intertidal zone, we need to talk about tides.

Tides are the changes in the ocean level caused by the gravitational pull of the sun and the moon coupled with the rotation of the Earth. The water in the oceans shifts around based on this. Some places experience one high and one low tide per day. Others have two of each. The area that is underwater at high tide but not underwater at low tide is known as the intertidal zone. The plants and animals that live here are very specialized. They constantly experience extreme changes in their environment.

The things living at the higher end of the intertidal zone are out of the ocean water the most. The things living at the lower end of the intertidal zone are underwater much of the time, but not always. Mussels, clams, and barnacles all live in the intertidal zone. Their shells help seal them up so they don't dry out when the water is at low tide. Then they open up to feed as water covers them.

Sometimes jellyfish, horseshoe crabs, and other sea critters get stranded on the beach as the tide goes down. Be extra careful; you might need an adult to help you, but you can return these creatures back to sea when this happens.

Have you ever heard of tide pools? Maybe not if you live far from the ocean. These are small, rocky depressions that water remains trapped in as the tide goes out. They are some of the neatest places to explore. Be careful you don't slip on the wet rocks, but everyone should get to take a peek inside tide pools before they grow up. Look for sea anemones with their tentacles shifting in the waves. Do you see any sea stars? Can you spot some crabs, or perhaps a fish, in the tide pool?

Don't just sit there on the beach. The intertidal zone is a favorite place in nature for people. Explore the plants and animals that call this dynamic landscape, and waterscape, home.

CRAB

Here's another animal that you're likely familiar with. At least it seems like you're familiar with it, right? This is probably because you see it on the menu of so many seafood restaurants. True, millions of crabs are consumed each year (people especially love crab legs), but there are many, many more species out there that never see a dinner plate. And all the different types are a pretty fascinating bunch.

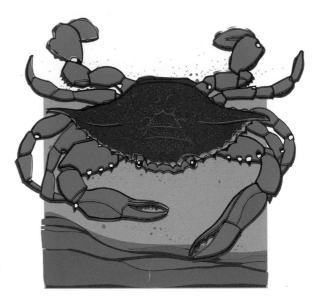

LITTLE-KNOWN FACTS

1. Crabs have five pairs of legs, so ten legs total. The most famous two are the top ones. They are considered the pinchers.
2. The horseshoe crab is not a crab at all. Instead, it is a closer relative to arachnids. Horseshoe crabs are still pretty amazing, though. You can check these out along the Gulf and Atlantic Coasts, especially when they come ashore in spring to lay their green eggs.

ANIMAL ALL-STAR: Giant Spider Crab

You can find this crab in the waters off Japan. If you see a picture of this crab, the first thing you'll notice is the long legs. In fact, spider crabs have the longest legs of any crabs—they can reach more than 12 feet from one end to the other. They can also weigh a whopping 40 pounds.

3. Have you ever heard that a crab walks sideways? It's true. Just take a look for yourself sometime. They actually swim sideways too!
4. Here's a fun fact: Want to know what a group of crabs is called? A cast!
5. A male crab is called a Jimmy. A female is called either a Sally if it's young or a Sook if it's an adult. Look at the shape of the apron on the underside of a crab. If it's long and skinny, the crab's a Jimmy. If it's shaped like a triangle, the crab's a Sally. And if the apron has a bell shape, it's a Sook.

Types: Thousands of species
Size: A few inches to several feet
Eats: Algae, worms, other crustaceans
Eats Them: Octopuses, fish, rays, turtles
Range: Worldwide

GO OUTSIDE

It's time to try your hand at crabbing! Even if you don't want to save the crabs to eat, catching them is still a fun experience. You'll want to go with an experienced person who can show you the ropes. Some people even use chicken necks as bait.

SQUID

A close cousin to the octopus, a squid might look like an octopus at first glance. Some might recognize squid more once they hear the word "calamari." If you think this sounds like something you eat, you're right. Calamari is a squid dish served at seafood restaurants, and it's very popular. In general, squid are a little easier to spot in the ocean because they'll swim around in the more open areas.

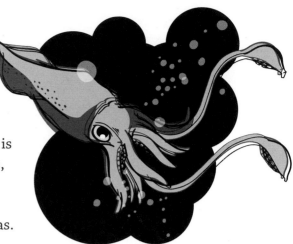

LITTLE-KNOWN FACTS

1. Like octopuses, squid can change their colors to adapt to their surroundings. This really helps them stay camouflaged against predators.
2. Also similar to octopuses, squid have eight arms. However, they have two additional tentacles, which are longer than their arms. These act like two arms almost, and they're what squid use to deliver food to their mouths.
3. A squid's digestive system actually passes through the brain. Isn't it weird to imagine what you eat going through the thing you rely on for thinking?
4. While most squid are a few feet long, the giant squid can be over 60 feet! They live deep in the ocean, so scientists know very little about them. But if you can imagine a school bus just floating around in the water, then this is about the size a giant squid would be.
5. Here's a cool thing to think about: Like other ocean animals, it can be hard to study squid. Scientists believe there are other species out there that haven't been discovered yet.
6. Both octopuses and squid have these little pits behind their eyes—this is where they smell!

Types: More than 300 species
Size: Varies greatly, from a few feet to dozens of feet
Eats: Fish, shrimp, other squid, humans
Eats Them: Sharks, fish, whales
Range: Several species worldwide

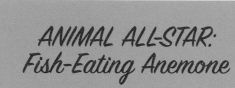

ANIMAL ALL-STAR:
Fish-Eating Anemone

What makes this anemone cool? Well you might take a hint from the name. Yep, you guessed it—it eats fish. As fish or shrimp get near this anemone's tentacles, it pulls them in to feed. As it feeds, the anemone gets bigger and bigger.

ANIMAL ALL-STAR:
Giant Ostracod

This cool creature is kind of like a cross between a clam (because its body is hinged like a clam's) and a shrimp. This is because it looks like a shrimp inside of the main body. It is sometimes referred to as the seed shrimp. Ostracods can completely close off their bodies so you only see their antennae sticking out. These antennae are important too. This is how they swim, by moving their antennae through the water.

OCTOPUS

With its eight massive and impressive tentacles, the octopus is a well-known marine animal. You're not likely to see one, though, unless you visit an aquarium. Why is this? Just take a moment to check out how an octopus lurks in the dark and rarely moves around. This is how octopuses behave in the ocean as well. They don't often come out in the open. Study that cool octopus at the aquarium; you'll definitely gain a whole new appreciation for this animal.

LITTLE-KNOWN FACTS

1. You might think birds are the only animals that have beaks, but octopuses do too. They need the strong beak to break open the hard shells of the prey they eat.
2. The eight tentacles of octopuses also have strong suction discs on them. This really helps them grab hold of their prey so it can't escape.
3. Octopuses have a unique defense mechanism. If attacked, they can release a type of dark ink from an ink sac. This looks similar to smoke in the water. It will distract predators so they can get away.
4. Octopuses have a unique siphon to help them move. This helps them propel (usually backward) through the water, much like a jet engine or an outboard motor. So if an octopus isn't crawling along the bottom of the ocean floor, it's jetting across with its cool propeller!
5. The largest octopus species is the Giant Pacific. It grows to more than 9 feet, weighs more than 600 pounds, and can be found off the West Coast of the United States.
6. Baby octopuses spend the first few months of their lives up on top of the sea. They are really vulnerable during this time, so they really have to watch out for predators. They eventually settle down at the ocean floor.
7. Octopuses have large and powerful eyes, similar to human eyes, which they use to spot prey.

Types: More than 250 types; the common octopus, the most prevalent, is found throughout the world.
Size: Most range from 1 to 3 feet.
Eats: Fish, shellfish
Eats Them: Sharks, large fish
Range: Worldwide

ANIMAL ALL-STAR: Johnson's Sea Cucumber

All sea cucumbers are pretty cool, crawling along the ocean (they look like a giant type of worm), eating whatever they can off the ocean's floor. These creatures can grow more than a foot long. They have a cool bit of defense: If something attacks them, they can shed their organs as a way of defense. Don't worry, they can grow those organs back again.

ANIMAL ALL-STAR: Brain Coral

Remember that coral is an animal and not a kind of plant. This coral looks fascinating because it has the twisty shapes and little grooves that make it look a lot like a human brain! Coral reefs are an important part of ocean life, and many are in danger. This is yet another area where conservation is absolutely necessary for the future.

SPONGE

For many years, sponges were considered plants instead of animals. After all, they don't really seem to do much at first glance. Though they might resemble a plant in looks, they are a unique water animal. They're also fun to look for during a visit to the ocean. They are common in tide pools, so get ready to gain a whole new appreciation for these plant lookalikes.

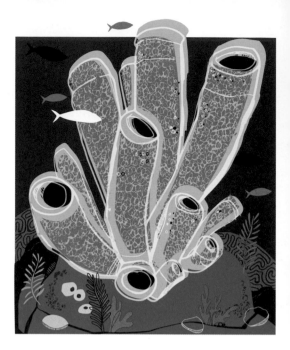

LITTLE-KNOWN FACTS

1. Most sponges are considered to be marine (saltwater) animals, but there are a number of freshwater species as well.
2. Sponges don't have many natural predators because they have a very tough texture and don't taste very good.
3. Sponge flies are specialized to feed on sponges.
4. Unlike most animals, which travel to get what they need, sponges are stationary. They stay in one spot and get everything they need right there. No wonder they get mistaken for plants. It really might seem like they are "planted" in one spot.
5. Sponges don't really have distinct body parts, or a skeleton, for that matter. Think of them as a large tube with the bottom closed off.
6. Sponges can vary a great deal in size. Some might be smaller than a penny, while others can grow to be bigger than a human.

Types: 10,000 species worldwide
Size: Varies greatly, from a few inches to several feet
Eats: Plankton and floating organic matter
Eats Them: Sea slugs, sponge flies, some starfish
Range: Worldwide

CRAYFISH

You can think of crayfish (often called crawfish in the South) as the lobster's little freshwater cousin. These water critters also go by names like crawdads, mudbugs, and fresh-water lobsters. Take one look at them and you'll see that they are similar in appearance to lobsters, with large claws at the front of their bodies. They are also popular pets, so look for crayfish in the next fish tank you see. You'll have the chance to observe them up close.

LITTLE-KNOWN FACTS

1. You can find crayfish in every state in North America, in Mexico, and in Canada. With hundreds of species, it's fun to see how many different types you can discover. Remember to look for differences, like claw shape, size, and color.

2. Nearly all crayfish burrow in the mud or silt along riverbanks and other bodies of water. This is good if you like to catch them. Lift up a rock, and you just might see a crayfish scurry out from under it.

3. Crayfish are very popular among people who like to fish. They will catch dozens of crayfish to eat.

4. You might think of antennae as something just for bugs, but crayfish have them too. They use their antennae to taste the water around them and to help find food.

5. Crayfish have special internal gills, though they can survive out of the water for an extended amount of time.

6. Crayfish build amazing tunnels, and the tops are called chimneys. Made of mud, they stick up out of the ground. The impressive tunnels can go several feet into the ground.

Types: Hundreds of species
Size: Usually a few inches, though some species much bigger
Eats: Plants, shrimp, dead fish
Eats Them: Raccoons, opossums, muskrats, many others
Range: Worldwide

GO OUTSIDE

Go on a crawfish hunt. This is a pretty common activity in the South, and you should experience it at least once. Some people use a pole to catch crawfish, while others use buckets or nets. Just remember to keep your fingers from their pinchers.

ANIMAL ALL-STAR: Copepod

Every animal has its place in the world, even if that place is being eaten by a lot of others. This is the case for copepods, which are tiny creatures just a couple millimeters. There are many different kinds, and the smallest can be microscopic. This kind of food is very important to whales and lots of other sea creatures, so it's good that we have these around.

LEECH

Leeches are like the vampire bats of the invertebrate world. And as you might suspect, this doesn't make them very popular with many people. They really can suck your blood (or the blood of animals) if you give them long enough to attach themselves. This is enough to make many people shudder, but try to look beyond that if you can. They are still pretty fascinating creatures, and they're part of our larger animal world.

LITTLE-KNOWN FACTS

1. Leeches have thirty-two to thirty-five body segments, and each segment has a brain segment in it, so it is almost like they have that many brains.
2. Leeches are considered hermaphrodites. This means they are both male and female.
3. If leeches had to, they could go quite a while without a meal. In fact, they could survive a year or two. This is because when they do eat, they really fill up.
4. Leeches are usually found in shallow, muddy areas. And, yes, they can attach themselves to you, but don't be afraid of going in the water. There are too many fun things in the water to be afraid of what might be inside. If a leech attaches to you, just pull it off.
5. Leeches are a lot like worms in many ways, but here's one big difference: They have suctions on both ends of their body where they attach themselves to people or animals. This is what makes them so effective, yet creepy too.

Types: More than 500 species
Size: Most are just a few inches, though some bigger species can get up to 12 inches.
Eats: Blood, worms, insects, some plant material
Eats Them: Fish
Range: Found around the world

LOBSTER

Lobsters are a popular seafood item all over the world. In fact, they are considered a really special treat for most people. The lobster fishing business is a huge one. It's a multi-million dollar industry. With their large, iconic claws, lobsters probably draw up a very specific image in your mind. This is a great start, but it is just the beginning.

LITTLE-KNOWN FACTS

1. To grow, lobsters shed their shells. They usually do this two or three times during their life.
2. You probably think of lobsters as being red, but they're not. Most of them are actually an olive-green color in the wild, but they turn red when they get heated up.
3. Here's a question you can trick your friends with: How many legs do lobsters have? They have ten.
4. Lobsters can and will attack (and eat) one another with their strong and powerful claws.
5. Most of the lobsters that are fished (more than 200,000 tons a year) are a cold-water species known as the American or European clawed lobster. However, there are dozens of other species, including both clawed and clawless species.

Types: Dozens of species worldwide
Size: From less than a foot to more than 3 feet
Eats: Fish, mollusks, some algae, plant life
Eats Them: Large fish
Range: Worldwide

SCIENCE Q&A: What Is the Continental Shelf?

The continental shelf is a bit of a confusing name. It's not really a continent. It's not really a shelf either. But once you know what it is, the name does make sense. So what is it?

If you think of a swimming pool, there is usually a shallow end and a deep end. The continental shelf would be the shallow end of the pool. It is the land that is under the ocean. The continental shelf extends out from the continents. The ocean is relatively shallow for a stretch before it gets rapidly deeper. The continental shelves are probably the result of earlier ice ages. They can extend from less than a mile to hundreds of miles out beyond the coast. For the most part the shelf is less than 500 feet deep at the edge. Beyond that, the ocean gets really deep, really quick. The continental shelf is wider along the Atlantic Coast than it is along the Pacific Coast.

The continental shelf is a super-productive area. Light can reach the ocean floor, allowing plants to grow. This allows numerous other species to thrive. Many of the marine invertebrates live along the continental shelf region, as do fish and marine mammals.

The ocean floor isn't flat. There are canyons and trenches, mountains and peaks. The shallow zone that borders the continents is the place to be, though, if you are an ocean critter.

STARFISH

Now is the name starfish or sea star? Both are acceptable names of this well-known ocean animal. What do you think makes them so popular? Maybe it's their shape, or maybe it's the way they attach themselves to things. You can often spot sea stars in tide pools and along shorelines, so be sure to keep your eye out if you're planning a trip to the seashore.

LITTLE-KNOWN FACTS

1. Many people think starfish are a type of fish, but they aren't. They don't have gills, scales, or fins. So don't make the mistake of putting them in the fish family.
2. Starfish can regrow parts of their body! For instance, if they lose an arm, they can regrow it over time.
3. Sea stars don't swim like a fish do. Instead, they move with the little tubes on their underside. These tubes act like little suction cups, and a single sea star can have hundreds of them.
4. Sea stars have a small mouth on their underside, but this doesn't stop them from eating larger prey. They can actually push their stomach through their mouth to eat something bigger—and then pull it back.

ANIMAL ALL-STAR: Bat Star

This is one cool sea star. First of all, don't expect it to have just five arms. It can have up to nine. Next up, it has a very cool way that it captures prey: When it finds prey with the sensors at the end of each arm, it moves over it. Then its stomach opens up and puts these oozy, gooey juices on top of its prey, turning it into a type of liquid. Then it eats it up.

5. You might think all sea stars have a classic star shape with five arms, but this isn't always the case. Sometimes they have several more arms. In fact, some have as many as forty!

6. If you look closely at a sea star, you'll see that it is very well protected. It has little spines on the top of its body, almost like protective armor, that keep it safe from predators.

Types: More than 2,000 species
Size: Can range from a few inches to more than 3 feet
Eats: Mollusks, including clams, oysters, and mussels
Eats Them: Sharks, rays, crabs
Range: Worldwide

GO OUTSIDE

Tide pools are a great place to explore. You can find all kinds of critters, including sea urchins and starfish if you're lucky. Remember, these star-shaped animals will use their little suctions to grab onto the side, so make sure you look closely.

ANIMAL ALL-STAR: Giant Isopod

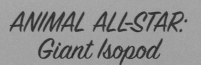

The giant isopod looks like an enormous beetle or some other insect. It's actually related to shrimp and crabs. Giant isopods like the deep waters of the ocean, and they can grow to be more than 12 inches. They mostly feed on dead fish.

SHRIMP

When you think of shrimp, you probably imagine some little pinkish-
white food that you eat, right? This
is true, and shrimp make really
popular meals. Actually, they're
not just popular meals to humans.
Shrimp get eaten by tons of animals.
They're just so small and easy to eat. Though
there's so much more to these animals.

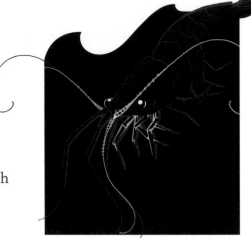

LITTLE-KNOWN FACTS

1. Female shrimp can lay 1 million eggs
   at a time.
2. Shrimps are crustaceans, which also include water fleas, crabs, and
   lobsters.
3. Prawns are animals closely related to shrimp. Many people have a tough
   time telling the difference, but the two have different gill structures.
4. Shrimp bodies are divided into two parts—a thorax and a head.
5. One thing that nearly all shrimp have in common is that they're found
   along the bottom of bodies of waters. They're generally fished in more
   shallow waters, but then they can be found 16,000 feet deep.
6. Don't think of shrimp as being pink. While it depends a great deal on
   species, most shrimp don't have much color to them at all—they're usually
   more gray. Like lobsters, they don't get pink until you heat them up.

Types: More than 2,000 species
Size: Mostly an inch or two, but some species are so tiny you can barely see
them.
Eats: Algae, plankton, tiny fish
Eats Them: Many predators, including fish, crabs, birds, sharks, humans, and
more
Range: Worldwide

SEA URCHIN

Sea urchins don't look much like an animal at first glance. They look like some kind of spiky plant instead. They are animals, though. You can find a few hundred species of sea urchins around the world, in all kinds of colors, so see how many different types you can spot. This is another animal that is common to see in tide pools, so keep an eye out.

LITTLE-KNOWN FACTS

1. Sea urchins often provide homes to other sea animals, like small fish and crustaceans.
2. Sand dollars, which are flat and shell-like, are actually a type of sea urchin.
3. Some sea urchins (like the flower urchin) have venom in their spikes. They use this as a form of protection, and it can definitely hurt human hands.
4. It's not uncommon for a sea urchin to live twenty or thirty years. The red sea urchin can live an impressive 200 years!
5. Sea urchins don't have a brain, but do they have a mouth? Yes! Their mouth is in the middle of the underside of their body. It even has its own nickname—Aristotle's lantern.

Types: Many different species, most shaped like a ball with spines all over their bodies
Size: Usually a few inches in diameter
Eats: Algae and small animals
Eats Them: Crabs, fish, otters, eels, birds
Range: Worldwide

GO OUTSIDE

Spend a day and just see how many different colors and types of sea urchins you can find. Make sure you know what you're looking for first. Then start looking!

MEET THE FISH

Fish make up a huge and fascinating family of aquatic animals. Who wouldn't want to spend their entire life swimming around underwater? Lots of things that live in the water aren't fish, though. So what makes a fish a fish?

All fish live in water, but they still require oxygen. Their gills let them get oxygen from the water. This is unique to fish, and it includes freshwater species like trout, bluegill, and walleye, as well as saltwater fish like sharks and marlins.

Here are a couple of other ways fish are unique. They are alike in that most have a streamline shape that helps them swim. Think about it—most fish do have similar shapes, whether they are big or small. Fish have other really cool adaptations that help them live in the water. For example, some have lateral lines that help detect vibrations in the water. Also, many have adjustable swim bladders that help them float higher or sink lower in the water.

To varying degrees, fish can see, smell, and hear too. Some fish, like gar, have large, heavy scales; others, like trout, have smaller scales. Other fish don't have any scales at all.

Fish have skeletons made of either bones or cartilage. Boney fish are the most common; some examples include salmon, catfish, pike, and many saltwater species. The cartilaginous fish are the sharks, skates and rays, and chimaeras. Lampreys and hagfish are a little different, and they get their own grouping—jawless fish. But they are still fish!

So there you have it. Trout are fish, and so are sharks. Fish are the most diverse type of vertebrates, with nearly 30,000 species.

EEL

Some people think eels are pretty odd-looking fish with long, snakelike bodies. You have to look past that, though. While these fish are mostly found deep in the ocean, they are still pretty fascinating Most eels are known for ambushing their prey—this means they lurk behind rocks and in the dark before they dash out to kill it.

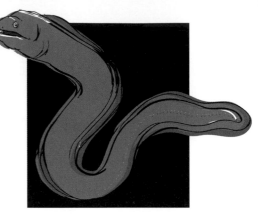

LITTLE-KNOWN FACTS

1. The pelican eel has an expanding stomach, so it can eat fish almost as big as its body!
2. Both pelican and gulper eels have a cool trick to attract prey: They have luminescent organs at the tips of their tails. This lures in curious fish so the eels can catch and eat them.
3. The avocet snipe eel is mostly found in semitropical areas of the eastern half of the United States. It has a unique look because its jaw can't shut all the way—so it looks like it's always open a bit. If you think about it, this can make the eel look kind of evil.
4. Eels can have more than one hundred vertebrae.
5. In general, scientists don't know a lot about eels. They are mostly deep-sea fish, so they don't get caught and studied a lot.
6. Lots of water snakes get mistaken for eels. People tend to call anything with a long body an eel, but don't make the same mistake.
7. Have you ever heard of the deadly electric eel that can deliver a shock strong enough to kill people? While this is a real animal, it's not actually an eel at all. It's more closely related to a catfish.

Types: A number of species off the coast of North America (mostly on the East Coast), including the avocet snipe, gulper, and pelican eel.
Size: Ranges a great deal. The pelican and avocet eels are both around 3 feet long; the gulper eel can be 5 to 6 feet long.
Eats: Small fish, crustaceans
Eats Them: Larger fish
Range: Most eels are found off the eastern coast of the United States; the pelican eel is also found along the West Coast.

SCIENCE Q&A:
What Is a Taxonomy?

In biology the naming and classifying of organisms is called taxonomy. Taxonomists don't just name new species, though. They also figure out how the different species are related to one another. Scientists look at the DNA of the organisms. Sometimes species can look almost identical, and DNA helps tell them apart. Other times organisms can look similar, but they aren't closely related at all.

Carolus Linnaeus and other scientists first started naming and ordering species in the 1700s. Taxonomists still use a similar order to classify a species. It goes from board categories down to each individual species. One way to remember the order is King Phillip Came Over For Good Spaghetti. Or you can come up with your own mnemonic. Like Ken's Pants Caught On Fire, Get Sprayer.

Kingdom
Phylum
Class
Order
Family
Genus
Species

Sometimes you'll see organisms referred to by their scientific names. (These scientific names are the genus and species names. They are always written in italics; the genus is capitalized and the species isn't.) Rainbow trout (*Oncorhynchus mykiss*) are the same genus, *Oncorhynchus*, as cutthroat trout (*Oncorhynchus clarkii*), but they are different species.

Taxonomists have named almost 2 million different species of organisms, but there could be as many as 30 million species, so there are plenty more to discover and describe. It is important to know the differences between the species and how they all relate to one another.

SHARK

Sharks are some of the most well-known and popular swimmers in the ocean. They are both celebrated and misunderstood. The popularity of sharks on television does show that people are curious about these fascinating creatures. But at the same time, many people consider sharks scary and dangerous, which usually just isn't the case. It's time to turn things around. Share these cool facts with people, and tell them not to be so scared of sharks!

LITTLE-KNOWN FACTS

1. Sharks lose teeth frequently, but there are replacements waiting. In fact, sharks can go through as many as 20,000 to 30,000 teeth during their lifetime.
2. Sharks don't have any bones. Even the legendary fin that people think of when they think of sharks is made up of cartilage.
3. While sharks have a bad reputation for attacking humans, this is actually rare. For instance, you have a better chance of being struck by lightning than getting attacked by a shark. By comparison, humans kill millions of sharks each year.
4. The whale shark is the largest shark (and fish) in the world. It can reach nearly 40 feet! This giant shark feeds mostly on plankton.
5. Three of the most dangerous sharks in the world include the great white, hammerhead, and tiger. All of these species are found in parts of North America.
6. While most sharks are pretty independent, some do form schools. The hammerhead species is one of these species.

7. You might not think of sharks as having a great sense of hearing, but they do. Through sound, they can detect prey thousands of feet away.
8. Scientists have evidence that sharks have been around for millions of years, and they were around when dinosaurs were.
9. There's a myth that says sharks must constantly swim to stay alive. While it is true that many sharks need to swim to force water over their gills as a way to breathe, they can take swimming breaks without dying.
10. A few of the sharks found in North American waters are the great white, sand tiger, bull, and leopard sharks.

Types: More than 500 species around the world
Size: Ranges a great deal, from a few feet to 40 feet or more
Eats: Mostly fish, but some will go after marine animals too
Eats Them: Not many predators other than people and killer whales
Range: Throughout the world, often near coasts

ANIMAL ALL-STAR: Zebra Shark

Zebra sharks like warm, tropical areas, so they are most common in the Indian and South Pacific Oceans. The zebra shark's signature look is actually spots instead of stripes. They are at the top of the food chain in the ocean and can live up to thirty years!

BASS

Bass are some of the most popular fish in the world. People who like fishing love to catch species like smallmouth, largemouth, and striped bass. There are all kinds of tournaments and records that people go after with bass. Luckily, it's not so hard to find them if you do like to fish. They are adaptable and survive in lakes, ponds, and streams.

LITTLE-KNOWN FACTS

1. Bass are in the sunfish family. They can be really beautiful too. So if you catch one or get the chance to see one up close, notice their colors or patterns.
2. Male bass have a strong role in the nesting process. The males build a nest for the females to lay eggs. Then the males protect the eggs until they hatch.
3. Bass are most active when it's warm. When it's colder, their metabolism slows down and they eat a lot less.
4. Bass do not have eyelids. Take a close look, and see if you can verify this for yourself.
5. "Otolith" is a weird word, right? Otoliths are the ear bones of fish. These help fish detect other fish and prey to eat.

Types: Around twelve species in North America
Size: Most are 16 to 24 inches.
Eats: Aquatic insects, crayfish, frogs, smaller fish
Eats Them: People, fish-eating animals like bears, eagles, raccoons
Range: Found in freshwater throughout North America

GO OUTSIDE

Challenge yourself to catch both a large- and smallmouth bass. First you'll want to know the difference between the two. If the mouth extends behind the eye, it's a largemouth. If it only goes as far back as the middle of the eye, then it is a smallmouth. Then see if you can catch both types. This is a fun challenge!

ANIMAL ALL-STAR: Guppy

Guppies go by a couple of other names too, including millionfish and rainbow fish. Originally from South America, today this little fish is very common and widespread as a pet fish. If you see a fish tank, there's a good chance you'll see guppies in it. Get a closer look and you'll be impressed by their vibrant colors.

ANIMAL ALL-STAR: Tuna

Tuna are probably one of the most recognized fish in the world because it's what you eat when you eat a tuna sandwich. This saltwater fish is a member of the mackerel family. They have systems that allow their inside temperature to be warmer than the water around them. This is unique among fish.

BLUE MARLIN

Marlins are some of the coolest-looking fish around because of their long, swordlike bill. They're so popular that the Florida Marlins baseball team has this fish as a mascot. If you don't have the chance to see these in the ocean, then make sure to stop by an aquarium in your area or when you're on vacation. You'll definitely be impressed. How can you not?

LITTLE-KNOWN FACTS

1. Blue marlins are very popular with people who like to fish because they are known for putting up a big fight when you hook them. They will sometimes even jump through the air.
2. Their long sword-shaped mouth is shaped this way for a reason: Marlins use this upper jaw to stun their prey.
3. Even though marlins can live deep into the ocean, they like to hang out on the surface, where it's warmer.
4. They aren't on the endangered list, but blue marlins are fished a lot, so scientists are encouraging people to conserve them. This can be accomplished by catching and then releasing them.
5. Marlins can get really big. They can weigh nearly 2,000 pounds. No wonder these giant fish can put up such a fight.

Types: The blue marlin is the largest member of the billfish family.
Size: Up to 14 feet
Eats: Mackerel, tuna, squid
Eats Them: Tuna, mackerel, sharks
Range: Eastern coast of the United States

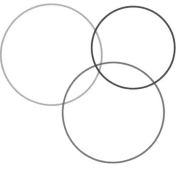

SKATE AND RAY

Skates and rays are a distinct group of ocean animals. They are similar in that they have flat shapes and long tails. While they don't always have the best reputation (blame it on the stingrays), they are pretty amazing animals. Of course the Mr. Ray character from the movie *Finding Nemo* has helped their reputation a bit. He was just so jolly!

LITTLE-KNOWN FACTS

1. Skates and rays will flap their fins like wings. However, it's slower, gentler flaps. You can often see this for yourself at aquariums where there's a ray exhibit. This movement helps them glide through the water and can also help rustle up their next meal.
2. A few species (like the manta ray) are filter feeders—they strain food through their mouths. Others have teeth made for crushing their prey.

ANIMAL ALL-STAR: Blue Skate

Also called the common skate, this is the largest skate in the world and can reach more than 8 feet! Even though they have "common" in their name, they are actually declining in numbers a great deal. They are mostly olive-gray to brown. So what's with the blue name? It's their underside, which is a lighter, blue-gray color.

3. What's the difference between skates and rays? They're very similar, but in general rays are more common in the tropics, while skates are found throughout temperate waters.
4. The largest ray in the world is the manta ray. It can reach more than 23 feet in length and weigh 2 tons! It's a plankton eater, though, so while it might look scary, in reality it's pretty harmless.
5. The rays that get a bad reputation are the stingrays, which can deliver painful—even fatal—shocks or stings with their tail. Just remember that, like most animals, stingrays won't bother you if you don't bother them.
6. Most rays and skates stick close to the ocean floor. They often blend in so well that it's hard to even see them.
7. Rays are generally pretty solitary animals, but there's a species called bat rays that gather in schools of hundreds.

Types: More than 600 species
Size: A couple of feet to more than 20 feet
Eats: Crabs, shrimp, lobsters, fish
Eats Them: Sharks, seals, other skates and rays
Range: Worldwide

GO OUTSIDE

Many aquariums offer the opportunity to touch rays. They are very gentle animals, and this is a really cool experience. Look for this opportunity in your area.

SEAHORSE

This creature might have a good chance of winning a sea popularity contest. With their long-snouted head, seahorses are fascinating-looking creatures. Because of their head and the bold shape of their belly, they do resemble a horse. They truly are some of the most unusual animals in the sea.

LITTLE-KNOWN FACTS

1. Most seahorse pairs are together for life. Male and females get together and then stick together for a long time. This is very unusual in the fish world.
2. Male seahorses have a pouch in the front of their belly where the females place the eggs. Then he carries them around until they hatch. That's right, the males are carrying those babies!
3. Seahorses are constantly eating. They might consume more than 3,000 shrimp in a single day.
4. There's a reason seahorse are constantly eating: They don't have teeth or a stomach, so food goes through them very quickly.
5. Some seahorses are endangered because of habitat loss and overharvesting. Many other countries use seahorses as an ingredient in medicines.

Types: Around thirty-five different species in the world
Size: From ½ inch to 12 to 14 inches
Eats: Plankton, tiny shrimp, algae
Eats Them: Crabs, stingrays, tuna
Range: In shallow, tropical waters throughout the world

DARTER

Did you know you can find rainbows underwater? Rainbow darters that is. Darters are small fish that are related to perch and walleyes. There are well over 150 species of darters. Some are found in just a few rivers and streams. Others are more widespread. The rainbow darter, for example, can be found in tributaries of the Mississippi River from Minnesota to Louisiana and east to Virginia, especially along the Ohio River Valley. But just because it is brightly colored doesn't mean it is easy to find.

LITTLE-KNOWN FACTS

1. Most darters are just 2 or 3 inches long. They aren't minnows though, just small fish.
2. Female rainbow darters aren't as brightly colored as the males.
3. The snail darter was the subject of early challenges to the Endangered Species Act. A lawsuit challenged a dam being built because it said it could wipe out this fish.
4. Some darter species are often indicators of good water quality.
5. Some darter species were not described until the 1980s, 1990s, and even into the 2000s.
6. Five species of recently discovered darters were named for political leaders who have championed environmental causes.
7. Candy, strawberry, cherry, lipstick, and brighteye are all species of darter.

Types: More than 150 species in North America
Size: A few inches
Eats: Invertebrates, algae, plankton
Eats Them: Larger fish
Range: Darters are common throughout North America; species vary by region

ANIMAL ALL-STAR:
Long-spine Porcupinefish

This fish has spines all over its body, which can make it look pretty intimidating. Also, it's among the group of fish referred to as blowfish because it can swallow water or air, inflating itself much like a balloon.

ANIMAL ALL-STAR:
Tropical Two-Wing Flying Fish

Flying fish? Yep, they really exist. These fish might look more like a dragonfly than a fish. They have these long fins that look a lot like wings. They often hang out around the surface of the water, and they'll jump through the air and then glide for short distances with their fins. You can find several species of flying fish in the world; this is just one of them.

CATFISH

These popular fish are like the cats of the fish world. Catfish have cool whiskers, which give them their name. Catfish are also a popular fish for eating. They can get really big, so people are always searching for those big catfish. There are actually many fish within the catfish family, but the channel, flathead, and blue catfish are some of the most well-known species in the United States.

LITTLE-KNOWN FACTS

1. Some catfish have sharp spines on their fins, so you have to be careful not to get poked if you ever catch one.
2. You might imagine catfish as being really big. Some are, but most average much smaller.
3. Most catfish have a head that is flattened. They also have whisker-like body parts outside their mouth that they use for touch and taste.

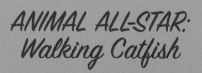

ANIMAL ALL-STAR:
Walking Catfish

This catfish of Southeast Asia has a reputation for "walking" across land from one area of water to another one nearby. Okay, it doesn't really walk. But it can move its fins to wiggle along. Still, this is pretty impressive for a fish.

4. Catfish are known for hanging out along the bottom of waters and in dark or murky areas.

5. While some catfish feed on other water animals, many are actually filter feeders. This means they filter out food like plants from the water.

6. Channel catfish generally reach 5 to 10 pounds, but they can get to be more than 40 or 50 pounds. These are the ones that anglers are after the most. (Psst! "Angler" is just a fancy word for someone who likes to fish.)

7. After a female channel catfish lays her eggs, she leaves and the male guards the nest.

8. Noodling is a common hobby in the South where people fish for catfish with their bare hands.

9. Some catfish are called bullheads.

Types: More than 3,000 species of catfish and their relatives
Size: Mere inches to several feet
Eats: Insects, clams, crayfish, worms, amphibians, other fish
Eats Them: Other fish, alligators, raccoons, bears, other fish-eating animals, people
Range: Worldwide

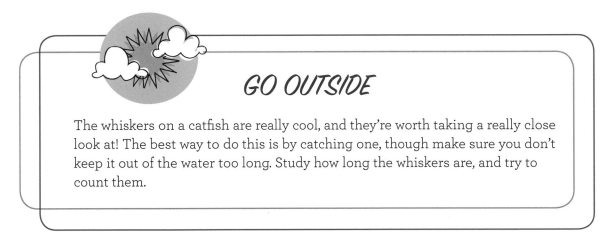

GO OUTSIDE

The whiskers on a catfish are really cool, and they're worth taking a really close look at! The best way to do this is by catching one, though make sure you don't keep it out of the water too long. Study how long the whiskers are, and try to count them.

PIKE

Pike are common fish in lakes throughout the North. They are fun to catch because they can reach sizes of more than 4 feet long. The next time you're in the northern part of the United States, try fishing for pike.

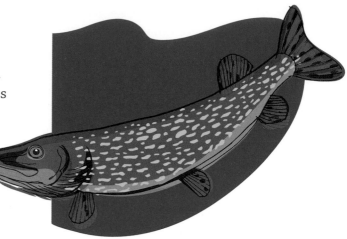

LITTLE-KNOWN FACTS

1. Northern pike have excellent camouflage, which helps them hunt.
   They lie in the weeds and wait for their prey to swim by. Then they rush out and attack.
2. The dorsal fin on the northern pike is located all the way in the back of its body. This also helps the fish attack prey because they can swim up without causing ripples.
3. Female pikes tend to grow faster and bigger than males.
4. Also in the pike family is the muskellunge, what many people know as a "musky." They can reach up to 6 feet and will feed on animals as big as muskrats. They are very popular with anglers.
5. Pikes have huge heads—about 25 percent of their bodies.

Types: One species, northern pike, in North America
Size: Up to 4 feet long
Eats: Frogs, bugs, smaller fish
Eats Them: Larger fish, fish-eating animals, people
Range: Throughout the Northern Hemisphere

SALMON

People love to eat salmon so much that there are salmon farms throughout the country. They are really good fish, and they are good for you too. This fish has more to it than just being tasty, though. They are important to ecosystems too. Lots of other animals depend on wild salmon for their own survival.

LITTLE-KNOWN FACTS

1. Salmon go into lakes and streams (freshwater) to lay their eggs. This is called spawning. Then after they hatch, they migrate to salt water. This makes salmon anadromous animals, living both in freshwater and salt water.

2. Salmon have very strong tails, which allow them to leap up waterfalls and get through other tricky areas to reach their spawning area.

3. The Atlantic salmon has a darker color in freshwater. When they enter salt water, they lighten and develop a silvery sheen.

4. Most salmon weigh less than 50 pounds, but the largest chinook (also called king) salmon can reach more than 100 pounds.

5. Sockeye salmon are known as red salmon because of the cool transformation they go through. Before they spawn, they have blue heads and backs. After, they have bright red bodies.

6. Here's another cool fact about salmon: They return to the place they were born, usually about four years later. They return to lay their eggs before they die.

7. Bears, eagles, and lots of other critters take advantage of the salmon, making meals of them as they move to their spawning waters.

Types: A handful of species around North America, including the Atlantic and five species along the Pacific Coast
Size: 3 to 5 feet
Eats: Plankton, smaller fish, water insects
Eats Them: Larger fish, fish-eating animals, people
Range: Mostly in northern, colder areas

GO OUTSIDE

Everyone should watch salmon spawning at least once. It's a pretty amazing natural occurrence, with hundreds of salmon swimming upstream at the same time. Find out if there are salmon in your area, then head to the river to see this for yourself.

SCIENCE Q&A:
Can Fish Live in Both Freshwater and Salt Water?

There are nearly 30,000 species of fish, and the species that live in freshwater are usually different than the species that live in salt water. But did you know that some species of fish can move between both salt and freshwater?

Fish that move in between salt water and freshwater are termed anadromous. Salmon are anadromous. The salmon life cycle starts and ends in freshwater. Adults stir up shallow depressions called redds, and eggs are laid here at the bottom of the stream. Young salmon hatch from the eggs. The adult salmon die in the freshwater after breeding and are fed on by lots of other animals, from shrews to bears.

Young salmon can spend a couple of years living in their freshwater stream before swimming downstream and into the open ocean. Salmon do most of their growing in the oceans. They stay out to sea for four or five years on average. Then they return back to the same freshwater stream that they were born in. They'll swim upstream for hundreds of miles before breeding and dying.

Steelhead are the same species as rainbow trout. Steelhead are similar to salmon, going between freshwater and salt water. Rainbow trout only live in freshwater, though. Cutthroat can also have sea-runs or live only in freshwater.

To add to the confusion, fisheries biologists have released salmon into some lakes that aren't connected to the ocean. These landlocked populations are popular for fishing. Kokanee is the freshwater version of the sockeye salmon. Other species of salmon can also survive in freshwater conditions.

TROUT

Trout are related to salmon and char. They are cold-water fish found mostly in freshwater. The most widespread native trout include rainbow trout, native to the western United States; cutthroats in the intermountain West; and brook trout in the Great Lakes and the East. They are also very popular among anglers. You can read all kinds of tips and tricks about the best way to catch trout.

LITTLE-KNOWN FACTS

1. Trout have teeth on the roof of their mouths; salmon don't.
2. Brown trout are native to Europe, but like other trout, they have been widely released to many nonnative habitats around the globe.
3. Rainbow trout that spend time in the ocean before returning to freshwater streams to breed are known as steelhead.
4. Cutthroat trout are named for the orange-colored slash marks under their jaws.
5. Rainbow trout have reddish or pinkish stripes along their sides.
6. The brook trout is the state fish of nine states: Michigan, New Hampshire, New Jersey, New York, North Carolina, Pennsylvania, Vermont, Virginia, and West Virginia.
7. Lake trout were historically a northern species. They are now causing problems in Yellowstone National Park because they were introduced there illegally. Now they outcompete the native cutthroats.
8. Darker backs and lighter bellies can create a camouflage effect for many species of trout.
9. The eyes on trout allow them to see above them, helping them avoid predators.
10. Fly fishers often try to mimic invertebrates and other trout food, while others prefer to do their fishing with worms or other bait.

Types: Dozens of species and numerous subspecies
Size: From a few inches to a few feet long
Eats: Fish, invertebrates, small mammals, aquatic vegetation
Eats Them: Fish, birds, mammals
Range: Throughout the United States

GO OUTSIDE

Trout species can vary a great deal from one area to the next. Do a little research to find out what trout are common in your state or region. Then put your family and friends to the test. How many different species did they know about?

ANIMAL ALL-STAR: Blue Tang

You can't mention *Finding Nemo* without talking about Dory. This type of fish is a blue tang. This fish is flat, and it can get up to 12 inches. The young fish are yellow—they don't get their signature bright blue color until mature.

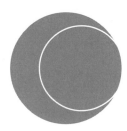

FLOUNDER

Flounder look more like pancakes than fish. They have flattened bodies and spend nearly all their adult lives on the bottom of the ocean floor. As larvae, flounders have eyes on both sides of their head. So they can say they have eyes on their back of their heads . . . kinda. As the fish grows, one eye slowly moves until both are on the same side.

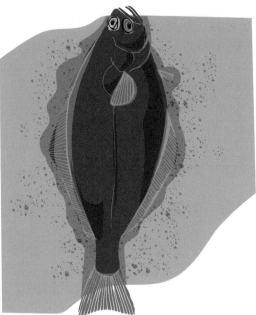

LITTLE-KNOWN FACTS

1. Flounder sometimes nearly bury themselves in the sediments at the bottom of the ocean to avoid detection by predators.
2. Some change colors to match their surroundings.
3. Summer flounder are also known as fluke, and they can be found off the Atlantic Coast.
4. Winter flounder typically have eyes on the right side of their bodies. Summer flounder generally have their eyes on the left side.
5. The top side of flounder is dark and sometimes spotted for camouflage, while the underside is pale.
6. Flounder often winter out in the deeper oceans and migrate to the shallower bays during the warmer seasons.
7. Like many other species, young flounder depend on the shallow coastal bays early in their lives.
8. Adults lack a swim bladder, helping them remain on the ocean floor.
9. Flounder are a popular fish for eating and can sometimes be caught from the beach.
10. Halibut are the largest flatfish species and are a right-sided flounder. They can weigh more than 100 pounds, and the largest approach 500 pounds.

Types: More than 700 species of flounder and relatives
Size: From 1 to 8 feet; most weigh a couple of pounds.
Eats: Fish, shrimp, squid, crustaceans
Eats Them: Other fish, dolphins, sharks
Range: Oceans and coastal bays

ANIMAL ALL-STAR: Clownfish

There are several different types of clownfish, and they can be red, orange, yellow, or even black. Some have multiple stripes (like Nemo and his dad), while others have just one stripe. Most are small, only reaching 3 to 7 inches.

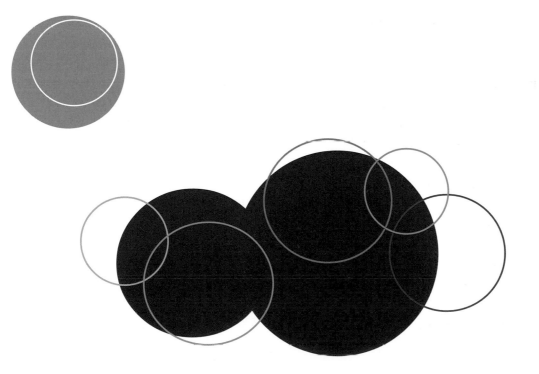

STURGEON

Sturgeons look like pre-historic fish, and they basically are. Sturgeons still look quite similar to related species found in early fossil records. They are prized for their great size and for their eggs. Caviar, a salty snack or spread, is traditionally made from sturgeon eggs. The decline in certain species of sturgeon is concerning, and many species are now protected.

LITTLE-KNOWN FACTS

1. Sturgeons don't have scales; instead they have bony scutes (plates) and denticles (toothlike projections) along their backs and sides.
2. The whiskers near the mouth of a sturgeon are called barbels, and they help the fish detect food.
3. Sturgeon mouths are like vacuums, sucking up food along the bottom of the stream or ocean.
4. Some sturgeons live in freshwater all the time; others are among the few fish species that breed in freshwater and then move to the ocean.
5. The shovelnose sturgeon has a nose that curves upward and looks a lot like a scoop. This is the smallest and most widespread species in North America, and you can find it in the Mississippi and Missouri Rivers.
6. Atlantic sturgeons used to be more widespread, but their numbers have been on the decline. Today restoration efforts are focused around the Chesapeake Bay.
7. White sturgeons live along the west coast of the United States and Canada and move inland into freshwater streams.

8. Technically, caviar comes from sturgeon, although fish-egg products are also sold from salmon, trout, whitefish, and numerous other species. The majority of sturgeon caviar is now collected from farm-raised fish.
9. The largest sturgeon can be almost 20 feet long.
10. Sturgeons can live a long time. In fact, the oldest can get up to 60 years old.

Types: About 25 species across the Northern Hemisphere
Size: Averages 6 to 12 feet
Eats: Crustaceans, mollusks, worms
Eats Them: Young sturgeon have a lot of predators, including anything that eats fish; adult fish aren't as vulnerable, but sharks are one of their top threats.
Range: Freshwater and coastal habitats

GAR

Gars are long, skinny fish with long, skinny snouts. They've been around since the time of the dinosaurs. Gars have specialized swim bladders that let them take in breaths of air. This helps them survive in areas with low dissolved oxygen in the water. If you've ever been in a swamp or a bayou and thought you saw a fish gulping up some air, there's a good chance it was a gar.

LITTLE-KNOWN FACTS

1. Gars are big predators, and they have very sharp teeth.
2. Gars tend to be long fish. The smaller species can reach 2 feet or more, while larger species can average closer to 4 or 5 feet.
3. Alligator gars are the largest species at nearly 10 feet long.
4. Gars have bony scales that are sharp, rough, and shaped like a diamond.
5. Gar scales were historically used as arrowheads, and the skin was used as body armor.
6. Gar eggs might be poisonous to mammals and birds, although more research is needed to understand this completely.

Types: Seven species
Size: Averages about 3 feet
Eats: Fish, invertebrates
Eats Them: Fish, alligators, birds, snakes
Range: North and Central America

WALLEYE

Walleyes (and the closely related sauger) are easily recognizable by their unique eyes. Their large eyes have special adaptations for gathering light, and they can look almost shiny. Walleyes are popular with the sportfishing crowd. They can be fun to catch and yummy to eat. There is also a large commercial fishery for walleyes, especially in the Canadian Great Lakes. In the wild they can live to be more than 20 years old, but 10 to 12 is more common. Still, this is pretty long for a fish.

LITTLE-KNOWN FACTS

1. The walleye is the state fish of Minnesota.
2. Port Clinton, Ohio, celebrates New Year's Eve with the annual walleye drop. It's kind of like in Times Square, only with a 20-foot-long, 600-pound fiberglass walleye being dropped instead of a ball.
3. Walleyes can live in lakes or in rivers. They often feed in the shallow areas at night and move to deeper water during the daytime.
4. The way to tell a walleye from a sauger is that walleyes don't have black spots on their dorsal fin (that's the spiky one on the back) and saugers do.
5. Walleyes and saugers sometimes mate with each other, and these hybrids are called saugeyes.
6. Walleyes were historically native to the midwestern United States and Canada, but now they are found throughout North America.

Types: One species in the world
Size: Most are about 2 feet, though the largest can be well over 3 feet and weigh more than 20 pounds.
Eats: Smaller fish, frogs, invertebrates, small mammals
Eats Them: Bass, pike, muskie
Range: North America

MEET THE HERPTILES

What exactly is a herptile? This is an interesting word that makes up an interesting group of animals. The group includes all reptiles and amphibians, even though they aren't really closely related. Perhaps they're lumped together because neither of them have hair or feathers. Either way, herptiles are really popular animals.

Reptiles and amphibians are some of the most familiar and most favorite animals. They can also be some of the most misunderstood. Lots of people love turtles, for instance, but not everyone is a big fan of snakes. Everyone should respect reptiles and amphibians, though. They are truly some of the most remarkable animals out there.

What are the differences between reptiles and amphibians anyway?

Reptiles include turtles, snakes, lizards, and the crocodilians. Once you look at reptiles, you'll see just how similar they are. Crocs and turtles might seem a lot different, but they both have dry, scaly skin. If you've ever held a reptile before, you know that reptiles aren't slimy at all, like some amphibians can be.

So what are other ways that reptiles are similar? Well, nearly all of them lay eggs. A few give birth to live young, but they're the exception to the rule. Also, young reptiles look like miniature adults, which isn't the case for amphibians.

Amphibians include frogs, toads, salamanders, and newts. Unlike reptiles, amphibians experience a major life change known as metamorphosis. To start with, they lay their soft eggs in the water, where they hatch. Young amphibians start their lives in water, and they look nothing like the adults. Think about how different tadpoles are from frogs. It takes them a while to change into their adult forms.

Amphibian adults breathe air, sometimes through their moist skin membranes. Also, while they don't have to live in the water as adults, they do need to stay damp.

So there you have it. Despite some shared characteristics like a lack of hair or feathers, reptiles and amphibians are quite different. There are about 6,000 reptile species and about 7,500 kinds of amphibians out there.

SCIENCE Q&A:
What Is Metamorphosis?

Amphibians and insects are the classics when it comes to metamorphosis, but there are a few other animals that also experience it. Metamorphosis is a great change. Sure, you will change as you grow up, but not like animals that go through metamorphosis. You pretty much look like your parents and all the other humans. Human babies are born with all the same parts that adults have. What about insects and amphibians though?

Let's start by examining frogs. As amphibians, frogs usually lay eggs in or around the water. These jellylike egg masses can include hundreds or even thousands of eggs. Not all these eggs will survive to become frogs, though. These eggs can be stuck to underwater vegetation or, in some species, just floating on the water's surface.

What hatches out of these frog eggs? No, it's not frogs, it's tadpoles. Tadpoles look more like minnows than frogs. They have a plump body, a tail, and no legs. For most species, the tadpoles live in the water for a few weeks; but some, like bullfrogs and green frogs, can remain as tadpoles for up to a year. Tadpoles swim around nibbling on algae and plant matter. They don't even have tongues yet. But they will.

Metamorphosis is a big change, and going from a tadpole to a frog certainly describes this. This change happens quickly too; it usually takes only about 24 hours. The tadpole tail is absorbed for nutrients, and frog legs grow. Tadpoles breathe through gills, while lungs develop for frogs to breathe with. Frogs tend to keep close to water, but they are no longer able to survive underwater like tadpole do.

This is only one example. Butterflies, moths, and plenty of other insects go through a complete metamorphosis (other insects have what's called a simple metamorphosis). Butterflies and moths start off as eggs. Each species of butterfly or moth lays its eggs on certain species of host plants. Caterpillars hatch out of the eggs. This is the larval stage. After growing bigger and bigger, the caterpillars form a chrysalis (for butterflies) or a cocoon (for moths). This is the pupae stage of life. Adults will emerge from their casings, and they look nothing like the caterpillars they started out as.

Isn't metamorphosis amazing? Can you imagine changing from a tadpole to a frog? Or going into a chrysalis as a caterpillar and coming out as a butterfly?

TORTOISE

Tortoises are like land turtles. They have dome-shaped shells that offer them protection from predators. Stout legs are built for walking along on the land and for digging out burrows. Tortoises mostly live in hot environments, so they often seek shelter underground. In fact, they can spend up to 95 percent of their life underground. All three species found in the United States have experienced population declines, so you might have a hard time finding these awesome animals. Spring can be the best time to see them as they are on the move looking for mates.

LITTLE-KNOWN FACTS

1. The desert tortoise is California's state reptile. (Not all states have a state reptile, but it's worth checking out to see if your state does.)
2. Desert tortoises can dig tunnels more than 30 feet in length. Gopher tortoises dig even longer tunnels, up to 50 feet long.
3. Desert tortoises sometimes spend the winter burrowed together in small groups.
4. Tortoise burrows can also serve as homes for more than 350 other animal species, including small mammals, snakes, toads, invertebrates, and even burrowing owls.
5. Like turtles, tortoises lay eggs. The female might dig for several hours before she is finally ready to lay her eggs.
6. Tortoise shells are made up of between fifty-nine and sixty-one bones covered in scutes (plates) made of keratin, similar to our fingernails.
7. Tortoises can live to be many decades old.
8. The average speed of a desert tortoise is 0.2 mile per hour.
9. Male tortoises will sometimes push each other around like sumo wrestlers.

10. Tortoises can store water in their bladders. It's a survival method. This way they can survive long periods without water.

Types: Three species in the United States, around forty worldwide
Size: Most are 8 to 12 inches.
Eats: Vegetation, including grasses, flowering plants, and even cactus
Eats Them: Coyotes, bobcats, ravens
Range: The southern half of the United States, from South Carolina to Southern California

ANIMAL ALL-STAR: Galapagos Tortoise

Get ready to be impressed because this large tortoise can live to be 150 years old! Of course, 100 is more common for these animals, but that's still pretty impressive. These tortoises have a very small range off the islands of South America, and they are endangered. They can be more than 5 feet long and weigh 500 pounds. They are gentle giants—like most other turtles, they live most of their lives sunning themselves and eating vegetation.

SNAKE

Snakes are some of the most misunderstood animal species out there. Don't write them off, though. They are cool. In total, there are about 3,000 different species worldwide. However, there are similarities among all of them. For instance, they all have long, slender bodies. Also, their scaled bodies aren't slimy like you might think. Instead, they are smooth and feel dry. Look for snakes sunning themselves along the road or trail.

LITTLE-KNOWN FACTS

1. Most snakes lay leathery eggs. However, in some species the eggs hatch inside the female snake. Then she gives birth to live babies.
2. Snakes don't have eyelids. This is one reason they can look intimidating. They aren't blinking at all.
3. Snakes' forked tongue helps them detect pheromones (chemical signals), so snakes are really smelling with their tongues! Isn't that fun? Go ahead and try it. Stick out your tongue and see what you can smell.
4. The shortest snakes in the United States are the blind snakes (also called worm snakes), and they can be just 5 inches long. The longest snakes in the United States are the indigo snakes, which can reach nearly 9 feet.
5. Snakes grow throughout their lives, but the rate slows down after they reach maturity. As they grow, they shed their skin.
6. Snakes can unhinge their jaws, which allows them to swallow large prey whole.
7. There are seventeen species of venomous snakes in the United States, but if you leave them alone, they'll usually leave you alone. Don't be scared of snakes, because snakebites are actually quite rare.
8. Some people think you can tell how old a rattlesnake is by counting the number of rattles, but this is a myth.

9. Snakes are popular pets, but you should never release a pet into the wild. Places like the Everglades in Florida have become home to numerous pythons and boas, and these nonnative species can damage the local ecosystems and animals that live there.

10. There are native boas in the United States. The rosy and rubber boas are two examples.

Types: 115 species in the United States
Size: From a few inches to many feet, though most around a couple of feet long
Eats: From small invertebrates to medium-size mammals
Eats Them: Birds, mammals, other snakes
Range: All continents except Antarctica

GO OUTSIDE

It's such a cool experience to find a snake's skin out in the wild. The skins can be fragile, so it isn't always an easy task to find one still intact. To increase your chance of success, look along rocks or crevices that snakes would crawl over while trying to shed their skin.

ANIMAL ALL-STAR: King Cobra

The king cobra is famous in many ways. It has a very distinct look, and it's often used in movies whenever they need a scary-looking snake. They are highly venomous snakes. One of the reasons they are so well known is because of their size. They can get more than 12 feet long, and they can raise their heads and bodies up, almost looking a human directly in the eyes. No wonder moviemakers use them when they need to scare people with snakes! These snakes are found in South Asia.

ANIMAL ALL-STAR: Green Anaconda

This is the largest snake in the world. It can reach lengths of more than 30 feet and weigh more than 500 pounds. The females are much bigger than the males. Anacondas are actually kind of clumsy when they are on land, so they're usually found swimming through the water. This is one of the few snakes that keep their eggs inside the female; then she gives birth to live babies.

LIZARD

Lizards are the most diverse group of reptiles, with almost 5,000 species in the world. They have dry, scaled skin, external ear openings, and eyelids. Some lizards can shed their tail—a handy trick if you are trying to avoid getting eaten by a predator. It can even grow back in some instances. Depending on where you live, lizards can be common in your backyard. They can be hard to spot, though, so maybe you've never seen one. It's worth it to seek one out to watch. Lizards can be quite fascinating.

LITTLE-KNOWN FACTS

1. Most lizards lay eggs, but a few species give birth to live young.
2. Not all lizards have legs. Legless and glass lizards don't.
3. Oklahoma was the first state with an official state reptile. Adopted in 1969, it is the common collared lizard. Other states with lizards as the official state reptile include New Mexico (whiptail lizard), Texas, and Wyoming (horned lizard for both).
4. The largest lizard in the world is the Komodo dragon, weighing a whopping 180 pounds and stretching to 10 feet long.
5. The largest lizard in the United States is the Gila monster, a mere 2 feet and 5 pounds. It's pretty small compared to that Komodo dragon!
6. Skinks are a kind of lizard that have extra-smooth scales.
7. Some lizards perform an action that looks like push-ups. This is a way to display themselves to another lizard (especially during mating season) or as a way to defend their territory.

Types: About 5,000 species worldwide

Size: Most are between 5 and 18 inches.

Eats: Varies among species, but can include crickets, caterpillars, and other bugs

Eats Them: Birds, mammals, other reptiles

Range: Throughout North America and the world, except in extremely cold places

GO OUTSIDE

Lizards can be hard to spot because they're often camouflaged against the background. They also are great about holding still, so you don't see them until they start to move. Make it a goal to go out and find a lizard before it moves. You'll need really sharp eyes. Look in the crevices of a house, a fence, or along the base of a stump.

ANIMAL ALL-STAR: Komodo Dragon

Earning top honors as the heaviest lizard in the world, Komodo dragons can get to be more than 300 pounds. They are huge as far as lizards go, reaching more than 10 feet long. Scientists didn't even know the Komodo dragon existed until about one hundred years ago. Today there are only a few thousand of the species left in the wild.

ALLIGATOR AND CROCODILE

If you want to sound like a true scientist, you can call crocs and alligators by this name: crocodilians. This is their collective name, and it represents the amazing twenty-plus species that have been around since the age of the dinosaurs. They tend to have a bad reputation to many, but they are magnificent large reptiles.

LITTLE-KNOWN FACTS

1. Crocodilians can close a flap of skin at the back of their throat. This allows them to capture prey with their jaws without water seeping down their throat.

2. Baby crocodilians often ride in their mother's mouth to get around. They also stay with their mom for several months or up to a year before they go out on their own.

3. In the 1950s the American alligator (found in the Southeast) was quickly becoming endangered because many hunted it for its skin. Conservation efforts have helped this species rebound, though, and it's doing much better today.

4. During incubation, the eggs of alligators are determined to be male or female by the temperature! If it's below 86°F, the hatchlings will be female. If it's above 91°F, they will be males.

5. For the most part, alligators are found in North, Central, and South America, while crocodiles are mostly found in Asia, Africa, and Australia, with a few species in Central and South America and even occasionally in south Florida.

6. Most crocodilians are freshwater animals (one exception is the saltwater crocodile in Asia and Australia, which can grow to more than 20 feet). If you want to see one in the United States, go to places like Texas, Florida, and Louisiana.

7. You mostly think of crocodilians in the water, but they can also climb. They might climb a tree to get a better view of the area.

8. The crocodilian bite is famous for being powerful and deadly, and it's easy to understand why. They have more than sixty teeth, and they bite down with a force of thousands of pounds.

9. Even though crocodilians can bite down with a huge force, they can't open with the same power. In fact, a crocodilian's mouth can be held shut with a rubber band.

10. Another tooth fact: These large animals go through a lot of teeth. They lose and replace teeth often. They could go through thousands of teeth in a lifetime.

11. Crocs and gators are excellent swimmers and spend a lot of time in the water. They can also hold their breath for an hour.

12. They have excellent hearing. When the young start to hatch from their eggs, the mothers hear this and go to check on them.

Types: More than twenty species throughout the world
Size: 5 to 20 feet
Eats: Fish, birds, small mammals
Eats Them: Anacondas, pythons, jaguars, leopards
Range: Worldwide

FROG AND TOAD

Frogs and toads are a common and welcome animal in backyards and alongside ponds and streams. It's just not summer unless you find a frog or a toad. They're fun to catch, examine, and then release to go hopping along their way. Check out some of these amazing facts about the thousands of species of frogs and toads in the world.

LITTLE-KNOWN FACTS

1. Unlike most amphibians, frogs and toads have no tail. They lose their tail while they are transforming from their larval (tadpole stage) to adults.
2. While frog and toad feet can vary based on needs, they all have four toes on the front and five on the back. Those toes can vary from being webbed (for good swimming) to long, fingerlike structures for climbing and gripping.
3. Have you ever heard frogs and toads call? It's definitely not just a *ribbit, ribbit.* Their calls are so varied and so cool! They are able to do this with vocal sacs. The sacs fill up with air, producing the sound.
4. Some frogs and toads have this amazing ability to freeze during the winter—for instance, the wood frog of North America. They slow down their metabolism and even form ice crystals inside their bodies. But the high levels of glucose in their bodies keep their organs from freezing completely.
5. Some of the deadliest animals in the entire world can be frogs. While you don't have to worry about poisonous frogs in the United States, they are out there. They're mostly found in tropical areas, like the brightly colored poison dart frogs of Central and South America.
6. This fact is both cool and gross: Most frogs shed their skin often—they'll even eat it!

7. A group of frogs has a really awesome name. They are called an army!

8. Frogs don't chew their food. They have to swallow it whole.

9. Frog and toad eggs vary a great deal—they can be distributed in the water, in large groups, or even sit on the back of a frog. In fact, a toad in Europe called the midwife toad has the male carry the eggs on his back.

10. We want to set the record straight about something. There's a myth that says you can get warts by just touching a toad. This is not true. You can't get warts by touching toads—or frogs.

11. Many people define toads as being more common on land, with rougher skin, while frogs spend more time around the water and have smoother skin. This isn't entirely the case, but it's a good rule of thumb.

12. Frogs don't need to drink water—they can just absorb it through their skin.

Types: More than 5,000 species worldwide
Size: Varies, mostly from 2 to 8 inches
Eats: Mice, birds, snakes, insects
Eats Them: Many predators, including birds and otters
Range: Lots of frogs and toads worldwide

GO OUTSIDE

It's fairly easy to catch a toad or a frog, so put your skills to the test in a different way. Catch a tadpole instead. You will probably need a little net to help you out. After all, they are tiny, and they move fast! Once you do capture one, take a closer look and imagine that thing turning into a frog.

ANIMAL ALL-STAR: Goliath Frog

This is the largest frog in the world. You might not believe it when you first see it—their eyes can be almost an inch wide, and they can weigh 7 pounds or more. This is pretty huge for a frog, considering most frogs can sit in the palm of your hand. Found in Africa, Goliath frogs like being near rivers.

ANIMAL ALL-STAR: Green and Black Poison-Dart Frog

These frogs are gorgeous, with a beautiful black-and-green pattern. Some people even know them as the mint poison dart frog. Whatever name you choose to use, one thing is for sure: You do not want to be on the receiving end of this frog's poison. Just a very small amount of poison can make a human's heart stop beating almost instantly. These frogs are less than an inch long, and you can find them in warm regions like Costa Rica.

SALAMANDER

Salamanders are grouped in with newts in the amphibian world. While they might look like a lizard at first glance, they are actually more closely related to frogs and toads. The range varies quite a bit, but you can find at least one type of salamander in much of the United States, so be on the lookout for these cool critters.

LITTLE-KNOWN FACTS

1. Some salamanders have an impressive ability to regrow parts of their body, including toes and tails. Sometimes they can do this in as little as two weeks!
2. Yes, salamanders look like lizards, but unlike lizards, they actually have smooth and glossy skin. They have to stay moist.
3. A salamander has a very long tongue for catching its prey. Some salamanders have tongues longer than their bodies!
4. Most salamanders have both gills and lungs, but there is a family of salamanders that don't have lungs at all. They breathe through their skin instead.
5. The mudpuppy is a type of salamander found in North America. They have feathery outer gills that are bright red and look like they are bleeding.
6. The largest salamander in the world is the Chinese giant salamander. It can reach more than 6 feet long!
7. The tiger salamander is one of the most widespread in the United States. It's one of the most colorful salamanders too, with yellow stripes and blotches across its body. Females can lay up to 7,000 eggs in a single season.

Types: Hundreds of species worldwide; more than a dozen in North America
Size: From a few inches to more than 40 inches
Eats: Frogs, leeches, insects, eggs, worms
Eats Them: Fish, reptiles, larger amphibians
Range: Small ranges, though species found throughout North America

ANIMAL ALL-STAR:
Fire Salamander

The fire salamander, found in Europe, looks a lot like the tiger salamander of the United States. Its colors are a way of warning predators that it is poisonous. The poison comes right from behind its eyes. Imagine your eyes telling something to "back off and leave you alone!" It sure works for the fire salamander.

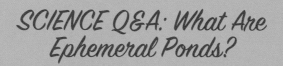

SCIENCE Q&A: What Are Ephemeral Ponds?

"Ephemeral" is a fancy term for something that only lasts for a short while. So ephemeral ponds are only ponds for part of the year, and then they dry up. They aren't just puddles of water though. Ephemeral ponds (sometimes called vernal pools) are essential habitats for numerous plants and animals that depend on these unique areas. These are really cool spots to explore.

Ephemeral ponds are usually low areas that collect melting snow or rainwater. They can be surprisingly deep, and the water might remain in them for many months. The water slowly soaks into the ground; some of it also evaporates. You might think that nothing could live in a pond that isn't a pond all year long. There are many species that are adapted to survive these annual wet and dry cycles, though.

Ephemeral ponds can be especially important to amphibians. Major movements of amphibians can occur in spring as the adults head to these ponds for breeding. They can lay their eggs in the ponds. These hatch out, and the larvae survive in the water. The larvae then go through metamorphosis and reach the adult stage. They then can breathe air and no longer need to live underwater, so it doesn't matter that their pond is drying up. Fish can be major predators of amphibian eggs and larvae, so one major advantage of ephemeral ponds for amphibians is that fish can't survive in them.

Amphibians aren't the only things that call ephemeral ponds home, though. So do lots of invertebrates, which the amphibians can feast on.

Spring is often the best time for exploring ephemeral ponds. It might be your only chance during the year to spot some salamanders or frog tadpoles. Put on some rubber boots, get out there, and explore.

GECKO

Known as snake lizards to many, geckos do look like a cross between a snake and a lizard. While geckos are not nearly as widespread in the United States as lizards, you will find them in the same types of areas, including rock crevices, up the walls of houses, and zipping about on the ground.

LITTLE-KNOWN FACTS

1. While most geckos don't have eyelids that function, the western banded gecko of the Southwest does have movable lids.
2. Without eyelids, most geckos lick their eyes as a way to keep them clean.
3. As a defense mechanism, geckos will shed their tail if they are captured.
4. Geckos have very special and powerful toe pads, allowing them to climb and hang on vertical surfaces. They can even cling upside down.
5. Many people think of geckos as brightly colored and imagine them changing color. While this is true for some species, most geckos are plainly colored in order to blend in at night.
6. Not all reptiles make a lot of sounds, but geckos use calls, chips, and even little barks to communicate with one another.
7. Female geckos lay soft eggs, often under leaves and bark. The eggs get harder as they are exposed to the air.

Types: More than 1,000 species worldwide; a small handful in North America, including the most common, the western banded gecko of the Southwest
Size: Averaging 4 to 6 inches, though some species can get up to a foot long.
Eats: Insects, spiders
Eats Them: Snakes, birds
Range: Small areas of North America, all in warm climates

ANIMAL ALL-STAR:
Kuhl's Flying Gecko

If you're familiar with a flying squirrel, then this flying gecko will make a lot of sense to you. It has flaps on either side of its body. And while it doesn't fly exactly, it can glide through the air, so it almost seems like it's flying. This little gecko is about 7 inches long, and you can find it in Southeast Asia.

ANIMAL ALL-STAR:
Panther Chameleon

You're going to have to plan a trip to Madagascar if you want to see this cool chameleon. It can reach 20 inches long, though females only get about half that size. The males are known for their cool ability to change their skin into flashes of color, which they use to attract females.

MEET THE BIRDS

Birds are everywhere. They inspire people with their ability to fly. They come in a rainbow of brilliant colors, and even the most simple brown birds can have glorious, detailed patterns. From the tiniest hummingbirds to the impressive condors, birds capture our imaginations. But what makes a bird a bird?

Feathers are the most recognizable feature of birds. Simply put, if an animal has feathers, it's a bird. If it doesn't, it's not. Feathers are remarkable structures, and one of their best functions is giving birds the ability to fly. However, not all birds can fly. And not everything that flies is a bird. For example, bats and bugs can fly too, but they don't have feathers.

Feathers have other tasks too. They can also help birds maintain their body temperature, communicate, provide camouflage, and lots of other things. Now feathers don't get the only credit for making it possible for birds to fly. Whether you're flying an airplane or are a bird soaring in the sky, weight matters. And birds have very lightweight bones to help make flying possible.

Another feature that helps define a bird is egg laying. There are other egg layers out there, but all birds definitely lay eggs. When they do lay them, the eggs must be kept warm until they hatch. Some baby birds, like shorebirds, hatch out and are ready to hit the ground running, but most still require much feeding and growth before they are able to leave the nest.

Birds don't have teeth, but they do have something that works just as well for them. Beaks (also called bills) come in a variety of shapes and sizes. Sparrows and grosbeaks have thick, heavy beaks for cracking open seeds. Hawks and owls have sharp beaks that let them tear bits of flesh from their prey. Some birds have long beaks for poking into the mud, like shorebirds, or for reaching deep into flowers, like hummingbirds.

So there you have it—the basics of what defines a bird. Of course there's still a wide range of bird types out there, nearly 9,000 species worldwide. Ready to learn about some of these cool flyers?

SCIENCE Q&A: What Are Other Signs of Animals?

Animals are a bit tricky. Many of them, like birds and squirrels, you'll see during the day, all the time. But there are many, many others that you might not see at all. Perhaps they come out mostly at night, or maybe they spend a lot of their time in the water. In either case, some animals are just hard to see. You have to look for signs of these animals to notice them.

What does this mean exactly? Well, you can look for their tracks and scat. This will help you know that there are animals in the area, and with a little practice, you'll be able to identify them. But there are a lot of other signs of animals that you might notice. Of course it helps to know what you're looking for.

Trees are a good place to start. Many animals use trees, and you can look for objects in trees or markings on trees for signs of animals. For instance, you can look for a nest up in a tree or a burrow along the bottom of a tree. You can also look for scratches, markings, or holes on a tree. Holes drilled all along a tree could be a sign of a woodpecker. Scratches might indicate where an animal climbed up a tree. Unexplained markings could be many other things, including a deer or a moose rubbing its antlers on the tree.

Aside from trees, also look for other signs of animals. This can include sticks piled up to make a den or home for animals. Don't forget to check water areas too. Sticks piled up in the water could be the makings of a beaver dam.

Once you start looking and noticing the area around you, there's no telling what you'll discover. So head outside and start exploring. Soon you'll start to see animals all around you.

SWAN

Swans often show up in literature. Remember the story of the ugly duckling that became a beautiful swan? Yes, these birds are known for their beauty and grace, but they can be fierce and even dangerous when it comes to protecting their young. Because of their large size, they have very few predators, and they can live for many years.

LITTLE-KNOWN FACTS

1. Not a lot of bird couples stay together season after season, but swans are known to mate for life. So the two swans you see this summer are likely the two you saw last year at the same time.
2. During nesting seasons, swans will aggressively attack animals or people to defend their young. If you come across swans with a nest or young, it's best to stay away.
3. Swans are known for their long, graceful necks. They have the most neck vertebrae of any bird, more than twenty in most cases.
4. A male swan is called a cob; a female is called a pen.
5. Swans were in danger throughout the 1800s because they were often hunted for their feathers.
6. Swans tend to live a long time. They've been known to live more than twenty years in the wild, which is longer than many other birds.

Types: Three species in North America—mute, tundra, and trumpeter
Size: Ranges from 50 to 60 inches
Eats: Grass, algae, insects
Eats Them: Not a lot of predators, though raccoons, coyotes, and other animals will go after them, their young, or their eggs
Range: Swans are found in small pockets of the country, wherever there is water. Tundra swans are found all around the coasts of Alaska and northern Canada.

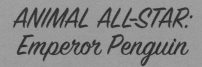

ANIMAL ALL-STAR:
Emperor Penguin

The emperor penguin of Antarctica is the largest of all penguins, reaching up to 45 inches tall. They have to endure extreme cold conditions, so they often huddle together in large groups to stay warm. Females lay an egg, and then they leave to hunt for up to two months while the male stays behind to care for it. These penguins dive deeper than any other bird—up to 2,000 feet—and they can stay underwater for 15 to 20 minutes at a time.

HUMMINGBIRD

Nicknamed "flying jewels" by many people, these tiny creatures are true wonders of the bird world. They are mostly known for showing up in summer, and there are oodles of fascinating facts about them. If you don't already love these teeny-tiny fliers, you will soon. You'll be putting out a sugar-water feeder to attract them.

LITTLE-KNOWN FACTS

1. Hummingbirds are the only birds that can fly backward.
2. A hummingbird's egg is about the size of a jellybean!
3. Though the hummingbird species in North America are limited, there are more than 300 species around the world.
4. The average hummingbird weighs about as much as a nickel.
5. A hummingbird's heart beats at a rate of more than 1,000 times per minute, which is nearly ten times the rate of most people! At rest, these birds also take about 250 breaths per minute.
6. In most species the male hummingbird is the one with the bright, flashy colors. They are the ones with the colorful red, purple, and blue throats and heads. Female hummingbirds are mostly green all over.
7. Hummingbirds have a long tongue, which they use to lap up nectar.
8. A hummingbird's nest is about the size of a golf ball. Hummingbirds lay an average of two eggs.
9. When it's cold, hummingbirds can conserve their energy by going into a state of torpor. This means they lower their metabolism and body temperature.
10. When flying, hummingbirds can reach speeds of about 30 miles per hour. When diving, that speed can be as high as 60 miles per hour.
11. The bee hummingbird (though not found in North America) is the smallest bird in the entire world. It's only a couple of inches long!
12. Hummingbirds are found only in the Western Hemisphere, so they aren't worldwide. This means you're not going to see a hummingbird in a huge part of the world, including Asia.

Types: More than a dozen species in North America.
Size: Very small, most only 3 to 4 inches
Eats: Lots of insects, nectar from flowers, and sugar water from backyard feeders
Eats Them: Larger birds, small mammals, even praying mantids
Range: The ruby-throated hummingbird is found in the eastern half of the United States. Other hummingbird species are concentrated in the West, especially the Southwest.

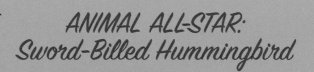

GO OUTSIDE

You can attract hummingbirds by mixing up four parts water to one part sugar. Make sure the sugar completely dissolves, and then put it in a sugar-water feeder. Don't add red food coloring to the water. It's not necessary, and it could even harm the birds. Late spring is the perfect time to attract hummingbirds.

ANIMAL ALL-STAR: Sword-Billed Hummingbird

If you ever get the chance to see a sword-billed hummingbird in person, you might think your eyes are playing a trick on you. This amazing hummingbird has a truly remarkable bill, which is about 4 inches long. This is longer than the bird's body! This beauty is found in South America, usually in areas of higher elevation.

DUCK

Lots of birds get lumped into the duck family, but you might want to be careful about lumping all water birds as ducks. For instance, grebes, loons, coots, and auks all look duck-like, but they are different bird families altogether. Ducks are often underappreciated too. It's easy to see ducks swimming on a lake or river, but you probably don't really pay them much attention. It's time to show ducks some respect!

LITTLE-KNOWN FACTS

1. Ducks are divided into dabblers and divers. The dabblers stay mostly on top of the water and just dip their heads in the water for food. But the divers actually dive down for food.

2. Ducks are another bird with males that are usually more brightly colored. For instance, the male mallard has a bright green head, while the female is brown overall.

3. You often see or hear about people who have pet ducks. These are usually domestic ducks, and they often look a bit different from wild ducks. Every once in a while, a domestic duck will escape, and you might mistakenly think you've discovered a new species.

4. Male ducks have a grand name. They are called drakes. Doesn't that sound like royalty?

5. Most ducklings take off and swim to the water almost immediately after hatching. They can be swimming within a few hours.

6. You know a duck quack sound? Well, not all ducks quack. Plus, it's often the female that is doing that familiar quacking. Most male ducks make a few sounds, but it's not the traditional quack we think of.

7. Ducks can keep one eye open when they sleep as a way to watch out for danger.

Types: More than thirty species in North America
Size: Many ducks are around 20 inches, but the size can vary.
Eats: Algae, plants, and insects; some ducks eat small water creatures, including some fish.
Eats Them: Birds of prey, snakes, turtles; people during duck hunting season
Range: Many duck species throughout the United States; most migrate, so they'll head to coasts in winter.

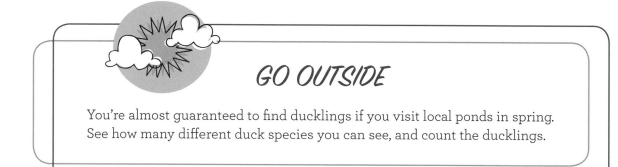

GO OUTSIDE

You're almost guaranteed to find ducklings if you visit local ponds in spring. See how many different duck species you can see, and count the ducklings.

HERON

Herons are large, graceful birds that are common sights along waterways in North America. If you like birds and are trying to share you love with others, then great blue herons are a good bird to show people. They are so large and graceful that they are really impressive. The great blue heron is the largest and most widespread heron, but there are other herons to be on the lookout for as well. They're all great at fishing, which can be really entertaining to watch.

1. Great blue herons stalk their prey. They go slow, are quiet, and are very patient. When they attack, they usually kill their prey with one quick, deadly blow of their bill.

2. Herons swallow fish whole. In fact, the fish can be much wider than the bird's neck, but it will still get down. Now this is something that would be awesome to see in person!

3. Herons often nest in trees in large groups. These areas are called rookeries, and they are so impressive. Ask around to see if there are rookeries in your area. It's worth the drive to see one.

4. Young herons can sometimes be aggressive with each other. They will even push each other out of the nest so they can be the dominant chick.

5. People used to hunt great blue herons for their feather plumes, which were used as decorations in hats. The heron population was definitely in trouble, but hunting herons was finally outlawed in the twentieth century.

6. Herons fly with their neck tucked in near their body, while cranes have their necks extended. This is a good way to identify herons when they're in the air.

Types: A handful of species in North America, including great blue heron, little blue heron, black-crowned night-heron, and green heron

Size: Ranges a great deal, from 13 inches for the green heron to nearly 50 inches tall for the great blue heron

Eats: Fish, small aquatics, reptiles, even other birds

Eats Them: Raccoons and large raptors like eagles and hawks

Range: The most common heron is the great blue heron, found throughout North America. Other widespread herons include the black-crown night-heron, found throughout most of the country, and the American bittern, a type of heron that is found throughout the country but is stealthy and seldom seen.

SCIENCE Q&A:
What Is Migration?

What do birds do in winter? They fly south, don't they? Or do they? Lots of birds migrate south for the winter, but plenty of others stay in the same location all year long.

Migration is a seasonal movement between areas. Some species fly a few hundred miles south, but others move to the tropics, thousands of miles away, for the winter. All the species that migrate need to have places to stop and rest along the way. They'll refuel with food and water. They might stick around for a few weeks, or they might just make a short pit stop. Then they continue on their journey.

Hummingbirds fly nonstop across the Gulf of Mexico on their migration, and blackpoll warblers fly for three days straight over the Atlantic Ocean on their way to South America. Migration can be dangerous and really hard on birds, so why do they do it? It often has to do with food, which is a pretty essential requirement. Birds fly to find the food they need to survive.

The arctic tern has the most epic migration. It flies from the arctic to near Antarctica and back every year. These elegant fliers can cover more than 25,000 miles each year. They basically follow summer around the globe. Much of this migration happens out over the ocean, but you can sometimes see them from the coasts or near other bodies of water.

Birds aren't the only animals that migrate. Some mammals also migrate. The caribou herds of Alaska and northern Canada make long migrations each year between their calving and wintering grounds. Some species of bats migrate south for the winter. Another flier, the monarch butterfly, is a champion migrator. Most head to Mexico or California for winter.

Some people mark the arrival of spring on their wall calendar. But people who like nature often define spring as the moment their favorite migrating bird returns from its southern wintering range.

EAGLE

This next bird is one of the most well known and respected in the county. The bald eagle is our national symbol, often associated with freedom and patriotism. All eagles are graceful, magnificent birds that never fail to impress when you see them in the wild. They always look grand, whether they're just perched or flying high in the sky. There are plenty of reasons to be impressed by these stunning birds.

LITTLE-KNOWN FACTS

1. Bald eagles return to the same nest year after year. Eventually the nest can weigh hundreds of pounds! So if you can find where a bald eagle nest is, you can see young bald eagles every year.

2. Eagles were in serious trouble in the 1950s because of a chemical called DDT, which really hurt these birds by affecting their eggshells. Today they are thriving once again, a true conservation success story.

ANIMAL ALL-STAR: Harpy Eagle

This beautiful eagle is commonly found in the rain forests of South America. It's considered one of the most powerful eagles in the world because it has massive talons measuring 3 or 4 inches. This might not sound like a lot, but it's the equivalent of bear claws. Females can weigh up to twice as much as males.

3. Bald eagles have that classic white head, but it actually takes them a few years to get it. When they are young, they are all brown, and they can often be mistaken for golden eagles.

4. All eagles can live a really long time. In the wild, they might live twenty or thirty years.

5. When they dive, eagles can reach a speed of nearly 100 miles per hour.

6. While most young birds leave the nest in a couple of weeks, eagles stay for about three months. Even when they do leave, they stick around the area, begging their parents to keep feeding them for a few more weeks.

7. Eagles are fierce hunters, but they'll also take a free meal. You might also see them scavenging for dead animals.

Types: Two eagle species in North America—the bald eagle and the golden eagle

Size: Both sit around 30 inches tall and have a wingspan of 80 inches.

Eats: Eagles feed on a wide range of both large and small mammals as well as reptiles, amphibians, and other birds.

Eats Them: Eagles are at the top of the food chain, and they don't have many predators as adults. Mammals will prey on the eggs or young.

Range: Look for bald eagles throughout North America; golden eagles have a smaller range, mostly in the West, but they will migrate to areas of the East.

GO OUTSIDE

Eagle nests can be a challenge to find, but once you do find one, you can usually find it again, year after year. Make this the year you find an eagle's nest, usually in the tops of trees. If you need help, reach out to your local bird club or Audubon organization to see if they know where one is in the area.

OWL

Owls fascinate people all over the world. They have gained a lot of popularity in the past several years, maybe in part because of Harry Potter. Actually, there have been lots of owl characters in movies and literature over the years. No matter how you think of owls, they are interesting creatures. They have reputations for being wise and mysterious. While this may or may not be true, they do have some pretty amazing abilities.

LITTLE-KNOWN FACTS

1. While owls mostly stick to themselves, a group of owls is called a parliament.
2. It might seem that owls can turn their heads all the way around, but that's not really the case. They can turn their heads about 270 degrees but not a full 360 degrees.
3. Some owls often have to survive in the cold because their range goes well into northern areas. One thing that allows them to do this is having feathers that go all the way down on their feet too.
4. Owls don't create (or excavate) their own nests out of trees. Instead they find nests that have been created by other birds.
5. They are one of the earliest nesters around. Many owl species will seek out a nest and lay eggs when it's still winter.
6. The eyes of owls are unique. They don't really have eyeballs like we do. Think of them as having long eye tubes instead that go way back into their heads.
7. Owls are fantastic hunters, and a big reason is because of their amazing hearing. They can detect prey animals from a great distance and then swoop in to kill them.
8. Owls have amazing feathers. They not only keep the bird extremely warm with great insulation but also help it be stealthy. You can barely hear owls fly. This helps them be great hunters.
9. All owls hoot, right? Not true. Some owls barely make sounds of more than a squeak.

10. Some owls nest in tree cavities. Owls in the Southwest will nest in cacti.
11. Owls don't chew their food. They swallow it bones and all. Later on, they cough up something called an owl pellet. This looks almost like a piece of poop, and it contains things the birds aren't able to digest, like teeth or claws!
12. Most owls are farsighted, so they see much better far away than right in front of them.

Types: Nearly twenty species in North America
Size: Varies a great deal, from the small elf owl (only 5 inches) to the great gray owl (27 to 30 inches)
Eats: Also at the top of the food chain, owls feed on a wide variety of small mammals, birds, snakes, reptiles, and more.
Eats Them: Few things eat owls, but other large raptors will, and mammals will try to eat their eggs or young.
Range: Owls are common throughout the country. The great horned owl is most common, found almost everywhere in North America year-round.

GO OUTSIDE

If not all owls hoot, what do they do? Go online and look up these three owls— great horned owl, screech owl, and snowy owl. You'll quickly see that owls don't sound alike at all. Now learn these sounds, especially of the great horned and screech owls. These are the two you're most likely to hear around your backyard.

ANIMAL ALL-STAR: Tawny Owl

The tawny owl is one of the most common and popular owls of Great Britain. It's on the small to medium size as far as owls go, roughly the same size as a pigeon. The males and females share parent duties. The female keeps the eggs warm until they hatch. Then the male takes over duties by bringing the young food such as small birds, voles, or even bats.

ANIMAL ALL-STAR: Red-and-Green Macaw

These birds are so beautiful that you might think they are pets instead of being out in the wild. These gorgeous red, blue, and green birds are the most common macaw, and they're fairly common in South American forests. Their huge bill can deliver a fierce force. This is good, since they need it to crack open hard nuts and seeds.

HAWK

Hawks are smaller than eagles, and you can find lots of them in your area, flying alongside highways and even showing up in backyards. Hawks can be both challenging and fun to try to identify. First test your skills when hawks are perched. Then if you want a challenge, test them out when they are flying. They are powerful, just like eagles and owls, and they definitely deserve your respect.

LITTLE-KNOWN FACTS

1. If you think eagles are fast, you'll really be impressed by hawks. Some species can reach speeds of 150 miles per hour when diving.
2. For many animals, the males are bigger. But this isn't the case with hawks. Females are larger than the males.
3. Hawks have hooked bills, which are very strong. They use these bills to tear flesh from their prey.
4. During mating seasons, hawks perform a mating ritual of acrobatic flight. This can last several minutes as the males try to impress the females.
5. Hawks have impressive eyesight. They can see prey (like a rabbit) more than a mile away.
6. If you have bird feeders in your backyard, you'll likely see a hawk stalking it sometime, waiting for an unwary songbird. Chances are you're seeing a Cooper's hawk or a sharp-shinned hawk. They are the most common backyard bird hunters.
7. If hawks have a big meal, they can go many days without needing to eat again.

Types: Around twenty different hawks in North America
Size: Most hawks range between 17 and 20 inches, with wingspans between 30 and 50 inches.
Eats: Small mammals and birds, reptiles, amphibians
Eats Them: Like other birds of prey, few things eat hawks, but they have to watch out for large mammals, especially when they are young.
Range: Hawks are found across the country, with the red-tailed being the most widespread, but be sure to look for other species in your specific area.

WOODPECKER

Several woodpecker species are common in the backyard, and they'll come to feeders to eat suet, peanuts, peanut butter, and seed. Go ahead and get to know your backyard woodpeckers. You might be surprised at how many different species you can attract. Beyond the backyard, though, you can find many other types of woodpeckers throughout the country. All the birds in this family have similar features and abilities.

LITTLE-KNOWN FACTS

1. Why do woodpeckers peck wood? It's usually either to dig out a hole for nesting or to search for bugs to eat. The drumming sound can also help establish territory and attract mates.

2. The tongue of a woodpecker can be two or three times the size of its head. Woodpeckers use this extremely long tongue to help them reach into trees to catch insects.

3. The name "woodpecker" is pretty literal—it means that the birds peck wood. They can peck up to twenty times per second.

4. The woodpecker's skull is unique because it has special air pockets. This allows their brain to be safe and protected from all of that pounding.

5. Most woodpeckers have zygodactyl feet, which means they have two toes in the front and two in the back. Of course there can be exceptions, like the three-toed woodpecker. This structure helps them grip onto trees and other surfaces.

6. You can see woodpeckers on every continent except Australia. Worldwide, there are about 200 species.

7. Woodpeckers have many different nesting habits. They nest in trees and birdhouses, and those in the Southwest also use cacti.

8. With many woodpecker species, the males have red on their heads while the females do not. Get a good field guide to see what you're looking for.

9. A couple of now-extinct woodpeckers were huge. The imperial woodpecker, for example, was nearly 2 feet long!

10. Sapsuckers are a type of woodpecker that drill in trees, looking for sap. You can find signs of their drilling by looking for several holes in a row on a tree.

Types: Nearly twenty species in North America; some of the most common include hairy, downy, and red-bellied woodpeckers.

Size: Woodpeckers range in size from the downy woodpecker at 6 inches to the pileated woodpecker at 17 inches.

Eats: Insects, nuts, berries; backyard feeders for suet and seeds

Eats Them: Larger birds and mammals that eat birds

Range: You can find a few different woodpecker species anywhere in North America, so find out which woodpeckers to look for in your area.

GO OUTSIDE

Woodpecker holes are all over backyards, parks, and woods. If you don't know what the holes look like, do a little research online first. Then go on a hike to see how many different woodpecker holes you can find. You could even make it a game and challenge your friends!

ANIMAL ALL-STAR: Green Woodpecker

At around 14 inches, this is the largest woodpecker in Great Britain. It's also gorgeous, with a beautiful green color. This woodpecker is a little bit different than most because it spends a lot of time on the ground. This is because it likes to feed on ants. It will even go back to the same anthill every day to eat. These woodpeckers can be a little shy, but their loud, laugh-like call gives them away every time.

WREN

You might not even notice wrens because they are mostly brown and plain looking. They are common backyard birds, and they will likely use a birdhouse if you put it out. (Not all birds use a birdhouse.) Take time to notice and appreciate these little birds. One sure way to recognize them is by their stiff tails.

LITTLE-KNOWN FACTS

1. Wrens might be little, but they can be fierce competitors during nesting season. They'll fight much larger birds to secure a spot for their young.
2. They might be small in size, but wrens have a very loud song. If you hear a loud, beautiful song in spring, there's a good chance it's a wren.
3. Nesting season starts in spring and goes through summer. Wrens raise two or three broods total in a single season.
4. Male wrens usually start building the nest. Then the female comes by to inspect it. If she likes it, they stay. If she doesn't, they move on to a different area to see if it suits her better.
5. If a house wren comes across another nest in the area where it's trying to nest, it will try to destroy the nest or peck holes in the eggs. Like many other birds, wrens are very territorial. They don't want another bird in their space!

Types: A handful of species in North America, including house, Carolina, marsh, cactus, sedge, canyon, and rock
Size: Most wrens are between 4 and 6 inches; the cactus wren is the largest at 8 inches.
Eats: Mostly insect eaters, but also eat seeds, fruit, and peanuts
Eats Them: Larger birds and mammals that eat birds
Range: Wrens are common throughout North America and will readily nest in birdhouses. The most common is the house wren, found throughout North America in summer and in southern areas during winter.

WARBLER

A lot of people don't even know warblers are around. Yet they are some of the coolest birds and get a lot of attention during spring migration season. This is when they come flying through North America from their wintering grounds. They sure are impressive with their bright, flashy colors. If you've never noticed these birds before, now is the time.

LITTLE-KNOWN FACTS

1. There are more than fifty species of warbler in North America.
2. Despite looking similar, the New World warblers, sometimes called wood warblers, are not closely related to the warblers of the Old World.
3. The yellow-rumped warbler sometimes goes by the nickname "butter butt."
4. The ovenbird is named for the dome-shaped nest it builds on the forest floor.
5. In the summer months, yellow warblers are widespread. Listen for their *sweet, sweet, sweet, I'm so sweet* songs near water or in shrubby areas.
6. Most warblers weigh only about as much as a ballpoint pen.
7. The blackpoll warbler is a champion migrator. They fly nonstop for three days from the mid-Atlantic states to the northeast coast of South America.
8. Prothonotary warblers nest in tree cavities and will even use nest boxes when placed in the swampy habitats they prefer.
9. Male and female warblers can look strikingly different or nearly identical.
10. Some species molt into drab feathers in the fall, making them extra tricky to identify.
11. Most warblers are specialized to eat insects. They migrate to the tropics for winter. A few, like the yellow-rumped warbler, can shift their diets to berries and will winter in the United States.

12. Brown-headed cowbirds sometimes lay their eggs in warbler nests. The warblers end up raising the cowbird baby at the expense of their own young.

Types: Dozens of species show up in North America. A few of the most common warblers are yellow-rumped, yellow, magnolia, and Townsend's.
Size: Vary, but most between 4 and 6 inches
Eats: Lots of insects, some nectar; a few will stop in backyards for fruit.
Eats Them: Larger birds and mammals that eat birds
Range: Warblers are migrants that start showing up in spring and then they leave in the fall. Peak warbler migration is usually April through early June. That's the best time to go out to find warblers near you.

GO OUTSIDE

Identifying warblers might seem tricky at first, but it really isn't. While there are many species in North America, pick out just a few to identify. You might start off with the yellow and yellow-rumped because they are most common. Go to your local park in April or May. You're almost guaranteed to see these bright yellow birds (or the bright yellow butt in the case of the yellow-rumped).

ORIOLE

With its bright orange feathers, you're not going to miss this bird flying through your backyard. Even though the females don't have the super bright colors of the male, they are still beautiful birds that catch the eye. Orioles are popular birds in spring, and you should be able to spot them in your backyard or at local parks. So get out there and start exploring.

LITTLE-KNOWN FACTS

1. Orioles are superb at building nests.
   The nests are intricately woven with materials like grass, horsehair, and grapevine. They hang down like a sock.
2. You might not realize it, but orioles are part of the blackbird family.
3. Many orioles don't have a good reputation with farmers. They love berries, and they can really damage a fruit crop.
4. People say that orioles are attracted to the color orange. This is why you'll see orange feeders to attract them to your backyard.
5. Oriole populations are stable right now, but they are strongly affected by insecticides. If people spray insecticides, this often causes the birds to die. So when you can, help support conservation efforts for this bird.
6. If you haven't had luck attracting orioles to your yard, you might want to find out when they show up in your area. If you can put out oranges and grape jelly right when they reach your area, you have a much better chance of bringing them in to visit.

Types: Though 8 or more species will show up in North America, the three most common are the Baltimore, Bullock's, and orchard.
Size: 7 to 8 inches
Eats: Insects, some seeds; will come to backyards for oranges and grape jelly
Eats Them: Larger birds and mammals that eat birds
Range: You can find at least one oriole species throughout most of North America, though they are tropical migrators, meaning they arrive in spring and leave in fall.

CARDINAL

Though the popular northern cardinal is found only in the eastern half of the United States, it's still one of the most well-known birds in North America. You can easily spot cardinals year-round because the male birds are so flashy with their vibrant red feathers. The females' red hues are more subtle, but they are still easily to recognize. When you see a male, there's a good chance a female is nearby.

LITTLE-KNOWN FACTS

1. The northern cardinal is the state bird of seven states: Illinois, Indiana, Kentucky, North Carolina, Ohio, Virginia, and West Virginia.
2. Female cardinals also sing. This is uncommon in the bird world, because males usually do the singing.
3. Cardinals can raise multiple clutches of babies each summer.
4. Young cardinals have dark beaks that turn bright red-orange by fall.
5. The massive bill helps crack open seeds and nuts. In addition to black oil sunflower seeds, some people attract cardinals to their feeders with safflower seeds.
6. Northern cardinals and pyrrhuloxias (desert cardinals) are closely related to the vermilion cardinal of South America. They are more distantly related to some bunting and grosbeak species.
7. Male cardinals can be quite territorial during breeding season and are sometimes seen pecking at their own reflections on windows.

Types: The northern cardinal is in the eastern United States; the pyrrhuloxia, or desert cardinal, is found in the Southwest.
Size: 9 inches
Eats: Insects, seeds
Eats Them: Larger birds, small mammals
Range: Northern cardinals are mostly eastern birds, so they aren't found in places like California or Montana; the pyrrhuloxia has a very small North American range in Texas, Arizona, and New Mexico.

ANIMAL ALL-STAR:
Lesser Flamingo

The lesser flamingo is a beautiful bird of Africa. Even though it can reach up to 3 feet tall, it's actually the smallest flamingo in the family. Unlike the greater flamingo, which you probably see in most zoos, the lesser flamingo has a black bill. These birds feed mostly on algae, which contain pigments that give them their light pink color. They'll sometimes feed on shrimp too.

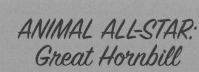

ANIMAL ALL-STAR:
Great Hornbill

The hornbill will catch your eye right away. It has an enormous bill in the shape of—you guessed it—a horn! The massive structure is used to attract females (yep, it's just the males that have this) and to possibly even fight with other males. They have an interesting nesting habit: They cover up the entrance hole to the nest. The female stays inside and the male pokes his bill through the hole to feed the female and the young.

KINGFISHER

If you have "king" in your name, you have to be pretty special, right? It's definitely the case with these birds. Kingfishers are common around water, and they are definitely impressive looking with their spiky crests and large heads. Listen for the rattling-chatter calls of kingfishers next time you are near the water. This is a bird that you'll likely hear before you see. So if you can learn its call, you'll get to see this bird even more.

LITTLE-KNOWN FACTS

1. Female belted kingfishers are more patterned than males. They have two stripes across their chest, a blue one and a brown one. Males only have a blue one.
2. Kingfishers nest in burrows dug into the earth. These burrows can be up to 8 feet long.
3. Baby kingfishers have acidic stomachs that help them digest fish bones and scales, but adult kingfishers need to regurgitate pellets of those no-longer-digestible materials.

ANIMAL ALL-STAR: Kookaburra

"Kookaburra" is just a fun bird name to say. Found in Australia, it's related to the kingfishers of North America. It's said that the call of the kookaburra sounds like a human laughing, echoing through the forest. Like the kingfishers here, you won't find this one too far from water.

4. There are nearly ninety species of kingfishers in the world. These cool-looking birds are really everywhere!
5. Kingfisher bills can have serrated edges like on a knife. This helps them get a good grip on their aquatic prey.
6. Not all species of kingfishers eat fish. Some in Africa even specialize in eating termites.
7. One of the most famous species of kingfisher is the kookaburra of Australia.

Types: Three species in North America—the belted, ringed, and green kingfisher

Size: Green kingfishers are the smallest (9 inches); next is the belted kingfisher (13 inches), and the ringed kingfisher (16 inches).

Eats: Fish, frogs, crustaceans, some insects

Eats Them: Large birds, raccoons, foxes

Range: The belted kingfisher is widespread and found throughout North America; ringed and green kingfishers have much smaller ranges, mostly in southern Texas.

GO OUTSIDE

Once you find a kingfisher (and they do have a wide range), just sit there and wait. Yep, wait for this cool bird to go diving down to the water to scoop up a fish. This is definitely worth watching at least once.

PELICAN

When you think of a pelican, the first thing you probably imagine is a bird with a huge bill, right? Well, this is true, but this isn't the only thing that makes these birds ultra cool. Look for pelicans around water, often near the ocean but sometimes far inland.

LITTLE-KNOWN FACTS

1. Although the average lifespan is much less, the oldest brown pelican lived to be 43 years old and the oldest American white pelican was more than 23 years old.
2. It might be tempting to think so, but pelicans don't actually store fish in their large bill pouches.
3. Flying brown pelicans feed by making a plunge dive into the water.
4. American white pelicans feed a little differently. They scoop up fish while swimming along.
5. Brown pelican populations have rebounded since the United States implemented pesticide restrictions.
6. Pelicans will something flap their throats and pouches. This is called a gular flutter, and it helps keep the birds cool.
7. They can incubate their eggs with their feet.
8. There are only about sixty total breeding colonies of American white pelican. One of the largest is on Yellowstone Lake in Yellowstone National Park.
9. Pelican species are found on every continent except Antarctica.

Types: Two species in North America—the American white pelican and the brown pelican

Size: White pelicans are roughly 60 inches, with a wingspan of 108 inches; brown pelicans are smaller, 50 inches and a wingspan of 84 inches.

Eats: Fish

Eats Them: Because they're bigger birds, they don't have a lot of predators, but an alligator or coyote would eat one if it could catch it.

Range: American white pelicans are found along the Gulf Coast, Florida, and California. They'll also go inland in specific areas of North America in summer and during migration. Brown pelicans mostly stick to the southern coasts of the United States.

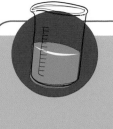

SCIENCE Q&A:
What Does Habitat Mean for Animals?

Animals all need the same basic things to survive: food, water, shelter, and space. Together these are termed habitat. Different species depend on different habitats, though. Let's take a look at different birds to understand this a bit more.

For instance, a mallard duck needs different food than a red-headed woodpecker. A screech-owl finds shelter in a tree cavity, while a roadrunner might seek shelter under a cactus.

You can help animals out by making sure they have protected habitats to live in. Animals might not get everything they need in your backyard, so this is where it's important to support conservation efforts. However, you can do a small part by adding valuable habitat right in your own backyard.

How? For starters, you can put up a bird feeder. Black oil sunflower seed will attract the most birds. You can also add some suet and some thistle feeders. Before long, you'll have a whole buffet for the birds.

Birdbaths can be a nice addition to a backyard habitat too. They aren't just for birds though. Plenty of squirrels, chipmunks, maybe even a raccoon after dark, will take a drink from the bath.

Shelter can take many forms for birds and other animals in your backyard. A simple brush pile can give animals a place to avoid predators and keep out of the rain or the snow. You can also put out homes for animals. Toad abodes can give shelter to toads. Nest boxes are popular for some bird species, including chickadees and wrens.

Space is a little trickier. It doesn't mean animals live in outer space. It just means that only so many animals can live in a certain area. Your whole town wouldn't fit in the grocery store, right? There wouldn't be enough space, and eventually you'd run out of food. The same is the case for birds and all animals. They need space, which is something everyone is after. Don't forget to support conservation efforts to preserve space so that future birds and animals have a place to live.

So all of that makes up habitat. No matter what species you're thinking about, food, water, shelter, and space are the essentials.

VULTURE

Vultures are superb scavengers. They will patiently search until they finally get what they need. In most cases, this comes in the form of food. Roadkill or any other dead beasts are favorite treats. You'll often see these birds gently flying overhead along roadways or perched with wings spread, but it's time to learn more about these birds that often have a bad reputation.

LITTLE-KNOWN FACTS

1. When vultures are soaring along without flapping their wings, you'll notice the wing tips are pointed up slightly, making a shallow V shape.
2. They use natural thermal air currents to fly along, circling higher and higher.
3. Young turkey vultures have black heads, while adults have red heads.
4. Vultures lack feathers on their heads, which is a great adaptation if you spend your life sticking your head in rotting carcasses.
5. Vultures, especially turkey vultures, have a keen sense of smell. This helps them locate their food.
6. Sometimes vultures come together in large night roosts.
7. Vultures have remarkable immune systems.
8. Black vultures are common from Mexico to South America. They are found in the southeastern United States and are expanding their range northward.
9. If they feel threatened, vultures will often vomit.
10. When they are hot, vultures defecate on themselves as a way to cool off. "Defecate" is another word for pooping. Birds don't actually have separate poop and pee. It's all the same.

Types: Two species in North America—the turkey vulture and the black vulture

Size: 25 inches tall, with a wingspan of 60 to 65 inches

Eats: Often feed on dead animals or carcasses on the side of the road

Eats Them: Few things eat vultures, but eagles or hawks will sometimes feed on the young.

Range: Turkey vultures are found throughout North America; black vultures are found mainly in the Southeast, but their range is spreading northward.

ANIMAL ALL-STAR: Palm Nut Vulture

Forget what you think you know about vultures. Palm nut vultures don't eat meat and others birds like other members of the vulture family do. This vulture mostly feeds on fruit of the oil palm. Sometimes it will eat seafood as well, but that's not its meal of choice. These large birds won't be found on roadsides like the ones we're used to here in the United States.

JAY

Jays have a reputation in the bird world of being bold and loud. After all, if you hear squawking outside or in your backyard, there's a good chance it's a jay. Most jays are large birds with bright, beautiful colors. They're also known for being very smart. But this is just the beginning of these fun birds.

LITTLE-KNOWN FACTS

1. Not all jays that are blue are blue jays. Steller's, scrub, and pinyon jays all have lots of blue on them too.
2. Gray jays can be especially bold. They are one of many species that have earned the nickname "camp robber," because they will sometimes steal food left out on the picnic table.
3. Pinyon jays are highly social and can live in permanent flocks of more than 500 individuals.
4. North America's two crested jays, the blue and Steller's, will sometime hybridize. This means two species mate together.
5. While most songbirds migrate at night, blue jays migrate in large flocks during the day. Look for them during spring and fall migrations.
6. The oldest wild blue jay known lived to be more than 17 years old.
7. The green jay is more common in South and Central America. It can be found in the United States in extreme south Texas.
8. In some species of jay, one-year-old birds will help raise the newly hatched baby birds.

Types: A handful of species in North America; most common are the blue jay, gray jay, and western scrub-jay.

Size: 10 to 13 inches

Eats: Seeds, nuts, insects

Eats Them: Larger birds and mammals

Range: You can find a jay in just about every part of the United States, though most species are found in either the East or the West.

GO OUTSIDE

Some people claim that if you hold a peanut out in your hand, you can get jays to eat right from there! If you're in an area with jays, you've got to give it a try. Remember: Patience is key!

ANIMAL ALL-STAR: Toco Toucan

The toucan might be one of the most recognized and popular birds in the whole world because of its large, bright bill. A lot of times it's the male with the much larger bill, but in this case, the male and female both have it. Their large, strong bill helps toucans eat young birds, eggs, and even lizards. They eat fruit too. Toucans nest in tree holes, and they often travel together in small groups of four to six.

ROADRUNNER

Roadrunners are common desert animals—you'll often seen them zooming across the desert looking for prey. As their name implies, you'll see them running alongside or across roads too.

LITTLE-KNOWN FACTS

1. Roadrunners are known for their speed. They can get up to nearly 30 miles per hour—not bad for a bird!
2. They have a very pointy—and deadly—bill. Roadrunners kill their prey by striking it with their bill.
3. Roadrunners know how to work as a team. They might join together to kill something like a rattlesnake. One bird will distract the snake while the other kills it.
4. They are really considered ground birds. They can fly awkwardly for short bits, but they mostly do everything on the ground, including nesting.
5. In many Native American and Mexican cultures, the roadrunner is a symbol of strength, courage, and endurance.
6. Roadrunners release salt out of a special gland near their eye. This helps them survive in deserts, where water can be limited.

Types: One species in North America—the greater roadrunner
Size: 22 inches
Eats: Lizards, snakes, birds, small mammals
Eats Them: Raptors, medium to large mammals
Range: This species is most common in the Southwest and into some parts of the central United States.

TURKEY

The wild turkey doesn't often get the respect it deserves in the bird world. Turkeys get the most attention around Thanksgiving time, but the wild turkey isn't like the domesticated turkey most people are eating for dinner. While they are big and a bit awkward for a bird, don't overlook this cool flier. Just take a look at some of these awesome facts.

LITTLE-KNOWN FACTS

1. In the early 1900s, turkeys were close to becoming extinct because they were overhunted. Conservation efforts helped them make a comeback, though. Today they are stable.
2. Male turkeys are called gobblers, while females are called hens. The males earned that name because of the gobbling sound they make.
3. Male turkeys have a couple of other things that the females don't. They have a beard (a long hairlike material) that hangs down their front. They also have tail feathers that they display, much like a peacock.
4. Turkeys will nest on the ground, but they often roost in trees at night.
5. Female turkeys are smaller than males by about 8 to 10 inches.
6. A lot of people think turkeys are bad fliers, but this isn't true. In fact, they can fly faster than 50 miles per hour.
7. Benjamin Franklin wanted the turkey to be the national bird instead of the bald eagle.

Types: One species in North America
Size: Up to 46 inches
Eats: Mostly ground feeders on seeds, other vegetation, even small bugs or reptiles
Eats Them: Coyotes and other meat-eaters
Range: Throughout much of the United States

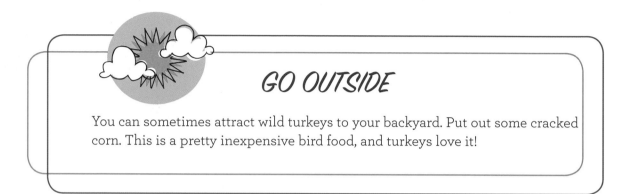

GO OUTSIDE

You can sometimes attract wild turkeys to your backyard. Put out some cracked corn. This is a pretty inexpensive bird food, and turkeys love it!

SPARROW

It's easy to lump all sparrows together. It's not hard to see why. Practically all of them have some sort of brown on them as well as streaking, so it seems like they are all pretty much the same, right? This is definitely not the case. Sparrows are a big bird family, and once you start noticing the differences among them, it can be really rewarding to tell one from another.

LITTLE-KNOWN FACTS

1. One of the most common sparrows in North America is the house sparrow. It's not a native species or even related to them. It was brought over from Europe in the 1870s. A lot of people don't like the house sparrow because it's aggressive, taking over nest boxes of bluebirds, wrens, swallows, and other birds.
2. The song sparrow is the most common backyard sparrow. You can find this bird all over the country during different times of the year. It has a lot of streaking along its front, and it's known for its sweet song, especially during spring.
3. Many sparrows spend their time out in fields (like the field sparrow). They like long grasses where they can hunt for plenty of insects and bugs.
4. Several sparrow species are declining because of habitat loss. The Henslow's sparrow and saltmarsh sharp-tailed sparrow are both examples of ones that are declining.
5. Two other fairly common backyard species are the white-throated and white-crowned sparrows. They look very similar, but the white-throated sparrow has a distinctive white throat.

Types: More than thirty species in North America
Size: Most 5 to 6 inches
Eats: Seeds, berries, insects
Eats Them: Hawks and other bird predators
Range: You can find several sparrow species anywhere in North America.

THRUSH

Just because a bird doesn't have the word "thrush" in its name doesn't mean it's not one. This is a bird family with a lot of variety, including the wood thrush, bluebirds, and the American robin. Of course you rarely hear someone call a bluebird or a robin a thrush, but they are still in this family. Now you can be among the people "in the know" of the birds in the thrush family.

LITTLE-KNOWN FACTS

1. During the 1970s, the bluebird population was in decline. Since then there's been a big effort to put up bluebird boxes so they have places to lay their eggs. It's worked too! The population is stable, and you can still put out a bluebird nesting box (there are specific size requirements) to help these popular birds continue to thrive.
2. Robins don't use a nesting box like bluebirds do. However, they do like platforms, and you can buy special nesting platforms for them.
3. Bluebirds and robins tend to be a "sign of spring" for many people, but you can sometimes find a few year-round if you look hard enough.
4. Brown-colored thrushes include the hermit, Swainson's, wood, and gray-cheeked thrush. These birds are hard to see deep in the trees and forests. They are fantastic singers, though, and are heard a lot more than they are seen.
5. Robins have some of the most easily recognized eggs in the world. They are light blue or greenish. There are usually 3 to 4 eggs total per nest.

Types: More than ten species in North America
Size: 7 to 10 inches
Eats: Mostly berries, insects, worms
Eats Them: Hawks and other bird predators
Range: Robins are found throughout North America; other thrushes are common too.

GOLDFINCH

Like the thrushes, the finch family is another tricky one. There are several birds in this family that do not have "finch" in their name. However, this time we're focusing on the goldfinch, which is one of the most recognized birds in backyards across North America. There's a lot more to them than their bright golden feathers.

LITTLE-KNOWN FACTS

1. Goldfinches aren't always yellow. They molt (old feathers fall out and new ones grow in) twice a year. So in wintertime, these birds are more olive-brown or green. Many people don't even recognize them.
2. Many birds feed their young insects and worms, but goldfinch babies just get seed. This is true for adults too.
3. Goldfinches are some of the latest to nest. This is so they have plenty of food (seeds) for their young.
4. A goldfinch nest can be woven so tight that it can hold water!
5. Males are the ones that are bright yellow, with the black on their head that looks like a cap. Females are more of an olive-brown color.
6. American goldfinches are found all over the country. If you want to see a lesser or Lawrence's goldfinch, you'll have to head to the Southwest. Both share the black cap of an American goldfinch, but their markings are very different beyond that.

Types: Three species in North America—the American, lesser, and Lawrence's goldfinch

Size: 4 to 5 inches

Eats: Seed

Eats Them: Larger birds, like hawks

Range: American goldfinches are most common and are found throughout North America; the lesser and Lawrence's goldfinch are both Western birds, with much smaller ranges

GO OUTSIDE

Goldfinches love thistle seed, which can be put in a special tube thistle feeder. This is a great bird feeder to buy, because squirrels usually stay away from it.

SWALLOW

The birds in the swallow family are among some of the best fliers in the entire bird world. You've probably seen them, even if you didn't know that's what you were looking at. They are always flying and swooping through the sky, snapping up insects. If a bird is zooming through the air and diving all about, then there's a good chance it's a swallow. Once you know their flying behavior, you can spot one from a long ways away.

LITTLE-KNOWN FACTS

1. The purple martin is a kind of swallow too. At 8 inches, it's much larger than the average swallow.
2. Purple martins nests in large groups. There are special birdhouses that look like a bird apartment with several compartments. Some people hang several gourds up to lure purple martins to stay and raise their young.
3. Barn swallows are common throughout North America. They're so named because they often built their nests up in the rafters of barns.
4. Other places where swallows build their nests include nooks and crannies of bridges and the eaves of houses.
5. Bank and cliff swallows will dig out a nest right in the side of a mud bank or a cliff. This is a pretty amazing accomplishment if you think about it. After all, these are only 4- or 5-inch birds!
6. Swallows have thin bills but really wide mouths for gulping bugs out of the air.

Types: 8 species common in North America

Size: Most species are 5 to 6 inches.

Eats: Insects, insects, and more insects

Eats Them: Larger bird-eating predators, like hawks

Range: Several swallow species found in pretty much any part of the United States

GO OUTSIDE

Learn to recognize the flight of a swallow. While in the air, it has a very distinct shape, and you can see how its tail sticks out. The way it swoops all about is unique too.

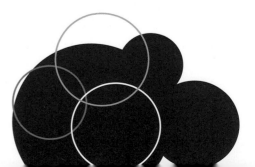

CHICKADEE

If you had a popularity contest for birds, the chickadee would make a run for the title. Sure, it might look like a plain, black-and-white bird at first, but these little guys are common all across North America. They are also often described as being friendly. No matter what type of chickadee you have in your area, these are pretty adorable birds that will surely go on your most-loved birds list. That is, if they're not on there already.

LITTLE-KNOWN FACTS

1. If it seems like chickadees are always coming to your feeder, it might be because they're taking the seeds off to hide them. They will hide (cache) seeds for later.
2. Many people have trained chickadees to eat from their hand.
3. Chickadees make a whistling call that sounds like *Cheeeeeeeese-Bur-Ger*. Listen for this sound when you're out and about.
4. Most chickadees travel in groups. So if you see one, there are usually more around.
5. Alaska has several chickadee species that the rest of North America doesn't see. Chestnut-backed, boreal, and gray-headed are all chickadees that you can only see in the far north.
6. If you head to the East, look for the Carolina chickadee. If you go to southern Arizona, look for the Mexican chickadee. There really are different chickadees in every part of the country!

Types: Seven different chickadee species in North America
Size: Most are right around 5 inches.
Eats: Seeds, berries, insects
Eats Them: Larger birds and bird predators
Range: The black-capped chickadee is the most common and widespread in North America. Others chickadees, like the Carolina, boreal, mountain, and chestnut-backed, have more-limited ranges.

MEET THE LARGE MAMMALS

Mammals are some of the most well-known animals in North America. They might be the most relatable, since people are mammals too. In addition, they are one of the most diverse groups. Just think about it—mammals include everything from a tiny shrew to a giant whale. Moose and moles have very little in common right? Wrong! They are both mammals after all. So what are some of the characteristics that make a mammal a mammal?

Mammals are vertebrates, so they have a backbone (a spine), but so do birds, fish, reptiles, and amphibians. What mammals have that these other critters lack is hair. Mammals all have hair at some point during their lives. It might just be a few rogue whiskers and some eyelashes, like with dolphins, but it is still there.

With the exception of those unique monotremes (more on that complicated-sounding word in the small mammal section), mammals give birth to live young instead of laying eggs. Another feature of mammals is mammary glands. This is how female mammals feed milk to their young.

So there you have it. Moose are mammals, and so are moles. With more than 5,000 species out there, it's time to get out and discover.

BEAR

There are three different bear species in North America. You have the widespread black bear, found from the swamps of Florida all the way to Alaska. You have the polar bears of the Alaskan and Canadian Arctic. Then there's the brown bear in Alaska, Canada, and other small areas of the northwest. No matter what species you're talking about, all bears are remarkable creatures. They are strong, powerful, and great survivors.

LITTLE-KNOWN FACTS

1. Did you think we were missing a bear because we didn't talk about grizzlies? They are actually the same species as brown bears.
2. Black bears aren't always black. They can be brown, cinnamon, or even blonde.
3. Black bear and grizzly bear cubs can stay with their mothers for up to eighteen months. Polar bears can stay together for nearly two and a half years!
4. Black bears and grizzly bears are omnivorous, meaning they eat both plant and animal matter. Polar bears have a more carnivorous diet, heavy in meat.
5. Ants and moth larvae can provide critical calories for bears, especially when other food is scarce. Grizzly bears will also dig up ground squirrels and plant roots with their long claws.
6. In preparation for hibernation, grizzly bears can gain up to 3 pounds of weight per day.
7. Not all bears actually hibernate. In warmer southern climates, black bears do not. They stay active, looking for food; they'll also climb trees.
8. Polar bears can travel more than 20 miles in a single day.

9. If necessary, polar bears can go for months without eating, surviving on their stored body fat.

10. Polar bear babies are about a foot long and weigh just a pound or so when they are born in the winter. They nurse on their mother's milk for many months before emerging from the snow den.

11. Polar bears will sit at a breathing hole, waiting for seals to pop up from under the ice.

12. Underneath all that gorgeous white fur, polar bears have black skin.

Types: Three species in North America—black, brown, and polar
Size: Most are 4 to 9 feet; they can weigh from 100 to 2,000 pounds.
Eats: Highly variable, including both plant and animal matter
Eats Them: Very few predators; they're most vulnerable when young, so mothers are very protective.
Range: Black bears are scattered throughout North America, brown bears are found in parts of the West up to Alaska, and polar bears are found throughout the Arctic.

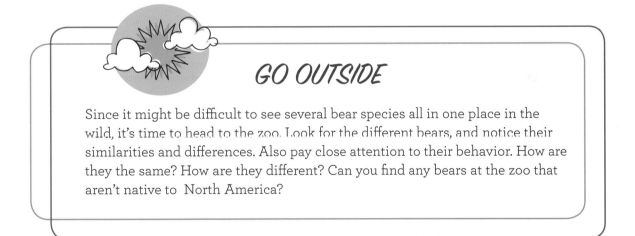

GO OUTSIDE

Since it might be difficult to see several bear species all in one place in the wild, it's time to head to the zoo. Look for the different bears, and notice their similarities and differences. Also pay close attention to their behavior. How are they the same? How are they different? Can you find any bears at the zoo that aren't native to North America?

SCIENCE Q&A: Do Carnivores, Herbivores, and Omnivores Have Different Teeth?

Lots of animals have teeth, but mammal teeth are some of the most impressive and specialized. For example, the teeth of mammals are deep-rooted and covered with a hard enamel surface.

While mammal teeth are similar in structure, there are many different types of teeth. Give yourself a big toothy smile next time you look in a mirror. Open up and look at those back teeth, too. Do they look the same as your front teeth? What about dogs and cats? Do their teeth look the same as yours?

Depending on what animals eat, the shape of the teeth can be very different. Carnivores are mostly meat-eaters. So you'll see that they have sharp teeth for shredding and cutting. Herbivores eat mostly plant materials. Their teeth are suited for grinding up plant matter. Omnivores eat a little bit of everything, so they have teeth that are able to chew both meats and vegetation. Nature centers often have skulls on display. Look for a herbivore skull (maybe a deer), a carnivore skull (perhaps a coyote), and an omnivore skull (like a black bear). What looks the same? What looks different?

Incisors are the front teeth. They are used to nip, cut, and bite. The first bite you take out of an apple is with your incisors. It's the same for animals. They'll bite off grass, a twig, a chunk of meat, or whatever else they eat. Rodents like mice and beavers have incisors that grow and grow. The gnawing they are known for helps wear their teeth down and keeps them sharp and chiseled.

Canine teeth are the long pointy teeth behind the incisors. Now these teeth aren't just limited to canine critters like dogs, coyotes, and wolves. Humans have them too. Human canines aren't that impressive, but carnivores can have major canine teeth. The upper and lower canine teeth can overlap when animals bite. This makes these teeth great for tearing off meat to eat. Some herbivores lack canine teeth, while others have stubby little canine teeth that aren't very useful. Walrus tusks are specialized canine teeth.

The premolars and molars are the back teeth. In herbivores, these are broad and flat. This helps them grind and chew on plants, which can be surprisingly difficult to chew up. In carnivores, the back teeth are sharp and pointy. They are like little meat tenderizers breaking down the meat. The carnassial pair is a set of teeth that fit together like the blades of scissors. Omnivore premolars and molars are shaped a little bit in between the teeth of herbivores and carnivores. This makes sense because they eat both plants and meat.

You can learn a lot about an animal just by looking at its skull and teeth. Scientists can tell different species based on their teeth. Sometimes they can tell how old individuals are too. So look for skulls to examine next time you're on a nature hike, or hit that local nature center and ask questions.

SEA LION

You might just think of one type of sea lion when you think of this animal, but there are actually six species in North America, which includes both sea lions and fur seals. They're counted in the same group because they are both eared seals, which means they have external ears. While you do have to live near the ocean if you want to see these animals regularly, they're worth a trip to the shore to see if you can spot them in the wild. The Pacific Coast is home to North America's eared seals, including the Steller's and California sea lions and the northern and Guadalupe fur seals. Otherwise, study these animals at the aquarium. These highly social animals can be fascinating to watch.

LITTLE-KNOWN FACTS

1. Populations of sea lions and fur seals are in serious danger, perhaps due to historic overhunting, declines in food sources, and shifting climates. We need to do our part to help conservation efforts for these wonderful animals.
2. They spend much of their lives at sea, diving deep to feed.
3. California sea lions can spend up to 20 minutes underwater.
4. Sea lion males have shaggy hair around the head and neck, similar but less obvious than a lion's mane. Males can also be four times larger than the females.
5. They can rotate their back flippers around, allowing them to walk on land. Well, "walk" might be a generous term, but you get the picture.
6. Sea lion males will vigorously defend the rocky coasts and protect multiple females during the breeding season.

7. Large gatherings of sea lions during breeding season are called rookeries. These can be really loud, with lots of grunting, roaring, and barking. Sea lions also have a loud, trumpeting alarm call when there is danger.
8. California sea lion males move north along the coast in the fall and winter.
9. Steller's sea lions are the largest species; they can weigh well over 1,000 pounds.
10. Their underfur can be up to fifty times thicker than land mammal hair. This, and a super-thick layer of blubber, helps keep the animals warm.
11. Some sea lions live in tropical areas like the Galapagos; others live in Australia and New Zealand.
12. Sea lions can swim up to 25 miles per hour.

Types: Six species
Size: 4 to 10 feet, 100 to 1,000 pounds
Eats: Fish, squid, octopuses, crabs, clams
Eats Them: Sharks, orcas
Range: Pacific Coast and Ocean

SEAL

The so-called true seals (as opposed to the fur seals and sea lions) lack external ears. They also can't use their flippers to support themselves like legs, so they hop and flop along when they are on land. They don't have to worry about this much, though. They spend most of their lives in the water, where they are excellent swimmers. On your next trip to the beach, look for a balloon-like seal head bobbing above the ocean surface.

LITTLE-KNOWN FACTS

1. Seals swim by flapping their hind flippers and using their front flippers as steering rudders.
2. If you see seals resting on land, this is called hauling. Be sure to give them plenty of space if you see this. Like other wild animals, it's best to keep your distance and not to disturb them—for your safety as well as theirs.
3. Seals have the ability to close their noses when they dive underwater.
4. Young seals are called pups. In large colonies of seals, mothers recognize their own pups by smell. Seal pups are pretty small when born, but they grow quickly by feeding on their mother's rich milk.
5. Females often don't eat while they are nursing their young. They must survive on their stored body fat.
6. It's true that you usually see seals in and around the ocean. Every once in a while, you might find one along a freshwater river, because harbor seals sometimes follow salmon upstream.
7. The rare Hawaiian monk seal only breeds in Hawaii and the nearby islands of the central Pacific Ocean.
8. Elephant seals are the largest seals (the largest males can weigh nearly 2 tons). Yes, they do have a trunk-like snout much like an elephant. Though only the males have this.

9. Ringed seals live in the far north. They will dig out snow caves for a place to rest. They are also a favorite meal for polar bears.

10. Hooded seal males can inflate an air sac as a display to impress female seals.

Types: Roughly thirty species worldwide
Size: Most are between 4 and 8 feet, though some can get up to 12 feet.
Eats: Fish, large aquatic invertebrates, seals, penguins
Eats Them: Sharks, orcas, polar bears
Range: Oceans and coasts worldwide

ANIMAL ALL-STAR:
Hippopotamus

The hippopotamus can float, swim, and dive down into the water for up to 5 minutes at a time. They can be fierce and vicious when it comes to defending their territory or young (called calves). They've been known to fight and win against other large, strong animals. You can find two species of hippopotamus in the world—the common hippo, reaching 9 feet and weighing nearly 1½ tons, and the pygmy hippo, only 5 feet and 600 pounds.

WALRUS

Even though very few people ever get to see them in the wild, the walrus is one of the most easily recognized species. Both the males and females have the iconic tusks. They are a North American animal, though you'll only find them in the extreme north. If you want to see one up close, your best bet it to hit your local aquarium or zoo.

LITTLE-KNOWN FACTS

1. Along with seals and sea lions, walruses are classified as pinnipeds. This means they are fin-footed.
2. As with other pinnipeds, the whiskers of the walrus are highly sensitive hairs called vibrissae. They have important functions, one of which is to help detect vibrations in the water.
3. The tusks of a walrus are a type of long canine teeth. They use their tusks to help pull their bodies out of the water and to chop breathing holes in the ice.
4. Males also use their tusks to display and attract females. Every once in a while, they will fight each other with them.
5. There are two subspecies of walrus, the Pacific and the Atlantic. As you've probably guessed, one is found along the Pacific Coast while the other is along the Atlantic.
6. Walrus pups sometimes "hitchhike" and get a ride on the backs of their mother.
7. The scientific name for walrus, *Odobenus rosmarus*, actually means "tooth-walking sea horse."
8. Walruses need thick skin to survive incredibly cold conditions. Their skin can actually be 4 inches thick.

9. Can walruses get sunburned? This might not be the right word for it, but their skin can change color. It's usually a grayish brown, but it turns rose-red if they bask in the sun.
10. Male walruses weigh about twice as much as females.

Types: One species (two subspecies), which can be found in extreme northern areas in North America and across the world
Size: 8 to 11 feet and up to 4,000 pounds
Eats: Mollusks, especially clams; shrimp; crabs
Eats Them: Polar bears, orcas
Range: Northern Pacific, Atlantic, and Arctic Oceans

ANIMAL ALL-STAR: Black Rhinoceros

Overall, there are five rhinoceros species in the world. Characteristics they all share include thick, tough skin and poor eyesight, but excellent hearing and smell. The black rhinoceros gets to be about a ton, though others can weigh up to 2 or 3 tons. All rhinos tend to travel alone or in pairs, and they all need help through conservation to ensure their long-term survival.

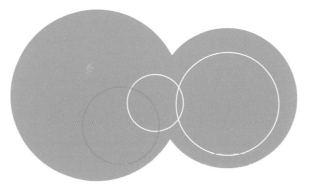

SCIENCE Q&A: Can People Really Identify Animals by Their Scat?

The short answer is yes. But first, do you know what scat is? "Scat" is a fancy word for animal poop. You might think that all poop looks alike, but that's not true.

Many people can just look at a pile of poop and tell you exactly what animal it came from. That's right, this is a science, just like identifying animal tracks. And, yes, there are books on scat—size, shape, type—as well.

It's easy just to say that large scat is from large animals and small scat is from small animals, but it's not as simple as that. So it's time to start practicing. What are you looking for? Notice the size—is it big or small? Next, notice the shape—is it all in a big pile or is it long and skinny? Maybe it's in pellet form, which is probably one of the most common scats in backyards around the county. (This is likely rabbit scat.)

If you're brave enough, grab a stick and poke around in the scat you find. Based on what you find inside, you might be able to tell what the animal has been eating. For example, if you find hair and bones in the scat, it's definitely from a meat-eater.

You probably never thought you'd be looking at and analyzing scat so much, but it's a pretty fascinating area of science once you start looking. If you can increase your ability to recognize animal tracks and scat, you'll definitely know what animals are in your area. This is a great skill to have, because chances are there are many more animals in your area than you think. You might not ever get the chance to see them in person, but it's satisfying to know that you can recognize their other signs.

MOUNTAIN LION

This species actually goes by many names. In fact, you might have thought these names were separate animals, but they aren't. The species name of the mountain lion is *Puma concolor*. Others names people use include cougar, panther, and puma. These are the most common names, but there are others as well, including catamount, ghost cat, sneak cat, screamer, and painter. The historic range of the mountain lion is from the Canadian north to southern South America.

LITTLE-KNOWN FACTS

1. Mountain lions are super athletes; they can leap 15 feet in the air and bound more than 30 feet.
2. They can reach 35 miles per hour for short stretches, so they often sit and wait for their prey. They might even stalk it. When they're ready to attack, they usually get what they want.
3. Pumas live in a wide range of habitats, which can include mountains, deserts, and forests. Maybe this is why they've gotten so many different names over the years.
4. Pumas use their tail almost like a rudder to help them maneuver quick turns.
5. The Florida panther is an endangered subspecies of the mountain lion.
6. Cougars don't roar like some other cats. Instead they can make scream-like noises that sound eerily human.
7. Baby mountain lions weigh less than a pound at birth. They have spots, which slowly fade away.
8. They are all born with blue eyes; their eyes turn yellowish as they grow up.
9. Mountain lions will partially bury uneaten prey so they can eat the leftovers later.

Types: One species, despite numerous different names
Size: 3 to 5 feet long and roughly 75 to 250 pounds
Eats: Will eat many other mammals, but they especially prey on hooved mammals like deer.
Eats Them: Young pumas can be targeted by wolves, bears, and other mountain lions.
Range: Northern Canada to South America

JAGUAR

The jaguar is the big cat of the Americas. Many people don't even realize that it can be found in the United States. It doesn't have a huge range here, though. The core of its range is South America throughout Mexico, but a few individuals venture north of the border into Arizona, New Mexico, and Texas. Jaguars are identified by their rosette patterns, but they are elusive and are rarely

seen. Still, they have a reputation for being fierce hunters, so people often do whatever they can to avoid encounters.

LITTLE-KNOWN FACTS

1. Not all jaguars have the signatures spots that you think of. Up to 6 percent of jaguars have dark fur and can appear almost black.
2. Though it's rare for cats, jaguars are excellent swimmers.
3. They can climb trees and sometime ambush prey species from above.
4. With their powerful jaws, jaguars can kill prey with a single crushing bite to the head.
5. Jaguars tend to drag their prey to a secluded spot before eating it.
6. They are solitary and will mark their territories with scat (poop) and scratch marks on trees.

7. Jaguar kittens are born naked and helpless, with their eyes closed. Females will defend them vigorously against predators, including other jaguars.
8. The only cats larger than jaguars are lions and tigers.
9. The home range of a male can be up to 50 square miles.

Types: One species
Size: Most are around 5 feet and weigh between 100 and 250 pounds
Eats: Deer, peccary, armadillo
Eats Them: Very few predators other than humans
Range: Extreme southern US border to South America

GO OUTSIDE

We don't have a lot of big cats in North America, but there are some pretty cool ones out there in the world. Do a little research and make a list of five other big cats. Then do a comparison on what makes them similar and what makes them different.

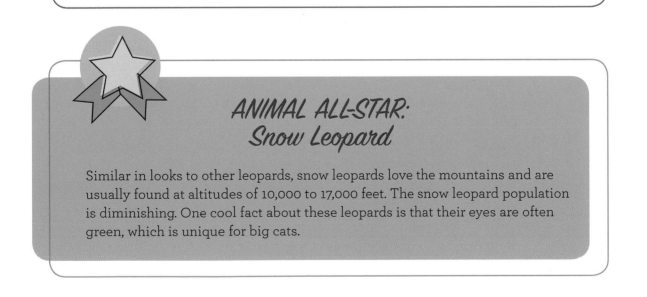

ANIMAL ALL-STAR: Snow Leopard

Similar in looks to other leopards, snow leopards love the mountains and are usually found at altitudes of 10,000 to 17,000 feet. The snow leopard population is diminishing. One cool fact about these leopards is that their eyes are often green, which is unique for big cats.

DEER

Deer are high on the list of wildlife that are somewhat easy to see. So if you're trying to increase your list of animals seen in the wild, try spotting a few different deer types. They are most active in the morning and at dusk, especially during the fall. Most deer populations are very strong. It's true that deer are popular among hunters, but here are a few things you might not know.

LITTLE-KNOWN FACTS

1. Does the white-tailed deer really have a white tale? It does, but it's mostly the underside of the tail that is white.
2. Male deer are called bucks; females are called does.
3. Mule deer sometimes hop along on all four legs like a pogo stick. This bounding is called stotting.
4. Breeding season for deer is called rutting. During this time, two bucks might face off, bellowing and behaving aggressively. If things escalate, the two deer will lock antlers to fight.
5. Deer shed their antlers in winter, usually by February. In spring they start to grow a whole new set.
6. Even though deer grow new antlers every year, they can still be a sign of age. Larger, more developed antlers can mean a deer is older. The antlers of really old animals, and those that aren't healthy, won't grow as big.
7. Moose, elk, and caribou are actually part of the deer family.
8. Baby deer (called fawns) are born with spots on their backs. They lose those spots when they're around 5 months old.
9. A "buck rub" is when bucks rub their antlers on trees or shrubs to mark their territory. When you're out on a hike, you can look for buck rubs a few feet off the ground.

Types: Two species in North America—white-tailed and mule
Size: Most around 5 to 7 feet
Eats: Plants, fruit, acorns and other nuts
Eats Them: Wolves, coyotes, big cats, people
Range: White-tailed deer throughout most of North America, mule deer in the West

GO OUTSIDE

Make it a goal to see a baby deer (called a fawn). It's really cool to see fawns in the wild, especially when they're really little and still have their spots, which will eventually fade. Sometimes the mother deer will hide her fawn in tall grass. If you come across one, you'll definitely want to keep your distance. Don't touch or approach too close.

ANIMAL ALL-STAR: Giant Panda

You've probably seen a lot of conservation efforts toward saving the giant panda, an animal found in China that can reach more than 6 feet. This is great, but the population is still not secure. These beautiful animals have a very restricted diet—they eat nearly 100 percent bamboo. Land has to be protected to keep these beautiful creatures around for future generations.

CARIBOU

Caribou are great migrators of the North. Some populations make one of the longest mammal migrations in the world and can travel more than 3,000 miles each year over the tundra. Others remain in the same forest all year long. They are popular, though. After all, Canadians put the caribou on the back of their quarter. Now that's a real tribute!

LITTLE-KNOWN FACTS

1. You want to know another name for caribou? Reindeer! Yep, they really are the same species.
2. They are the only deer species in which both males and females grow antlers. Males shed their antlers in late fall, while females don't shed theirs until well into the winter.
3. Baby caribou (called calves) can stand shortly after they are born, and they can keep up with their mothers just days later.
4. Caribou calves lack the spots that most babies in the deer family have.
5. The forests of northern Idaho and eastern Washington once had a sizable population of caribou, but today they are extremely rare there.
6. Caribou feet are extra large. This keeps the animals from sinking too deep in wet conditions, and the feet act as snowshoes in winter.
7. Their hollow hair helps insulate caribou. They also have adaptations in their noses that helps them breathe in cold air. This is because their nose hairs are short so they don't get frozen.
8. You might not think of these animals as being great swimmer, but they do just fine in the water.

Types: Numerous subspecies throughout northern North America
Size: Around 4 to 5 feet and about 250 to 600 pounds
Eats: Grasses, forbs, lichen
Eats Them: Wolves, bears, golden eagles
Range: Throughout northern North America

GO OUTSIDE

You don't have to travel to the cold and snow to see reindeer. These animals have become popular pets. They have even been domesticated in some areas. Look in your area to see if there is an animal farm or somewhere else where you can visit reindeer and see them up close.

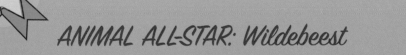

ANIMAL ALL-STAR: Wildebeest

Wildebeest travel in large groups in Africa, moving from one place to the next, wherever they can find a good source of food. While it looks like a cow, and even has cow-like horns, the wildebeest actually bleats like a lamb. It is considered a type of antelope, and its prized horns can reach up to 32 inches long.

SCIENCE Q&A: What's the Difference between Horns and Antlers?

Many people substitute the terms "horn" and "antler" with each other, but did you know they are really two very different things? If you see an animal sporting some headgear, how can you tell if they are horns or antlers?

To start with, horns are features found on cows, sheep, goats, and their relatives. In these species, both males and females can have horns, and they can be short or long. They can grow straight out like on mountain goats, or they can curl around like on bighorn sheep. They don't have forks, branches, or tines, though. They are a single beam. Animals that have horns keep them for their entire lives. They grow and grow. In some species you can see grooves that represent each year of growth, but this isn't always the case. Horns are made up of a bony core growing from the skull. They are covered in a sheath made of keratin, kind of like your fingernails.

The pronghorn, sometimes called pronghorn antelope, is a unique animal. It has horns, but as the name suggests, the male's horns have small prongs on them. Female pronghorn also grow horns, but they are short and smaller and don't show the same prongs.

Antlers are found on deer and their relatives, including elk, moose, and caribou. With one exception, antlers are found only on the males of the species. Do you know which species has antlers on both males and females? (Psst! Look for the caribou entry.)

Antlers can be single tines, usually called spikes, but they can also have lots of points. Elk and caribou have long, skinny antlers. Moose have broad, flat antlers. It is especially impressive to know these antlers grow back every year. They grow quickly during spring and summer. At this time, they are covered with fuzzy-looking blood vessels, and people call them velvet. The antlers reach their peak size in the fall, when they play an important role in mating displays. The antlers fall off (called shedding) in winter. These shed antlers are often nibbled on by mice and other critters.

Horns and antlers can be impressive sights. How many species can you find with horns? Have you ever found a shed antler?

ELK

For many people in regions where elk live, the bugle of a bull elk is a true representation of fall, just as much as the changing of leaves. Seeing elk in the wild is often a highlight for many who visit national parks in the West. Yellowstone National Park and the Tetons are both popular spots to see elk. Put it on your list to see elk in the wild if you haven't done so already.

1. The piercing bugle isn't the only sound elk make. They also grunt, bark, and even squeak to communicate with one another.
2. Tule elk are a subspecies found in central California; Roosevelt elk are a subspecies of the coastal Northwest.
3. Early elk relatives had longer, tusklike teeth (similar to a walrus). The elk of today have an upper pair of canine teeth that are sometimes called "ivories," which some people use to make jewelry.
4. This great animal used to be a lot more common throughout the country. There have been many conservation efforts to reintroduce elk back to their former habitat. This means relocating wild elk from one area to places where they used to be common but are now gone. This has been successful in some areas, and they're still working on it today.
5. Male elk are called bulls, females are called cows, and the young are called calves.
6. Another name for elk is wapiti, which means white rump.
7. Historically there were more than 10 million elk in North America; today the number is closer to 1 million.

Types: One species
Size: 4 to 6 feet and 400 to 800 pounds
Eats: Vegetation, shrubs, tree bark
Eats Them: Bears, wolves, mountain lions
Range: United States and Canada

GO OUTSIDE

It's not enough just to see an elk in the wild. You should also make it a goal to hear one bugle! First make sure you know what you're listening for. Do a search online to hear an elk's bugle—then you'll be ready.

MOOSE

Moose are the largest members of the deer family, but their gigantic size doesn't mean they are easy to spot. They often do a great job of hiding themselves in dense willow thickets. Or they might be swimming in ponds, and you won't see them at all. The next time you're hiking in moose territory, keep your eyes peeled. Once you finally do spot one, it'll be well worth the wait. These are one cool animal!

LITTLE-KNOWN FACTS

1. The species called moose in North America (*Alces alces*) is actually referred to as elk in Europe.

2. Only bull moose grow antlers, which can be more than 5 feet from tip to tip and weigh more than 40 pounds.
3. The antlers are broad and flat like the palm of a hand; they have numerous points sticking off of them like fingers.
4. Moose have a strange flap of skin hanging down below their throats called a dewlap or bell. This might be used to display dominance, or it might help cool moose off in summer. Nobody is entirely sure what function it serves, though.
5. Sometimes moose will stop eating for a bit in winter and just stay in one spot. This is a survival method, because they'd use more energy searching for food than the energy the food would provide.
6. Moose are very comfortable in the water. They feed on plants underwater and can remain underwater for 30 seconds or more.
7. Moose can be found in every Canadian province, so Canada is a very popular place for people who want to see moose in the wild.
8. Moose are so adapted to the cold that they sometimes overheat in summer.

Types: One species
Size: 8 to 10 feet and 600 to 1,300 pounds
Eats: Vegetation of all types
Eats Them: Wolves, bears, other large predators
Range: The northern regions around the globe

GO OUTSIDE

This might be the hardest challenge in the whole book! Moose can be hard enough to see on their own, but now go on an antler hunt. Can you imagine going on a hike and finding giant moose antlers in the woods? Cool!

BISON

Historically abundant and widespread in the American Great Plains, bison were overharvested for their meat and hides in the 1800s. Now bison can be found in numerous state and national parks, including Yellowstone in Wyoming, and Wind Cave and the Badlands in South Dakota. You can also see them in Wood Buffalo National Park in Alberta. A handful of people have domesticated bison (much like ranching cattle), but there's nothing like seeing these large creatures in the wild.

LITTLE-KNOWN FACTS

1. In the early 1900s there were only about 1,000 bison left in North America. People knew they had to help, so they started working to protect them. Bison populations have increased since then, but they will never be as abundant as they used to be.
2. They might be big, but they can still move. They can reach speeds of nearly 40 miles an hour.
3. Both males (bulls) and females (cows) have horns. The bulls' horns are thicker and larger than the cows'.
4. Bulls will use their horns in a face-off. They will head-butt each other, trying to establish dominance or fighting for a female.
5. Even though they aren't related to the buffalo of Asia and Africa, bison are sometimes called buffalo.
6. In winter the large muscular hump and big head of bison help them plow snow from side to side to find food.
7. Bison sometimes wallow, leaving large divots of dirt where they roll around.
8. One species of prehistoric bison had horns 7 feet across.

Types: Two species—one in North America and one in Europe
Size: 7 to 12 feet tall and 800 to 2,000 pounds
Eats: Grazes grasses and forbs
Eats Them: Bears, wolves, other large predators
Range: In parks, refuges, and preserves in western North America

ANIMAL ALL-STAR: South American Tapir

Tapirs have earned the nickname of "living fossils." This is because research shows that they have changed very little in the past 35 million years. There are four species of tapirs in the world, and they all look a bit piglike. The South American tapir uses its long, snout-like nose to eat grasses, fruits, and other vegetation.

ANIMAL ALL-STAR: Bactrian Camel

One of two camel species in the world, the Bactrian camel is considered critically endangered in the wild. These animals are fascinating because they can drink up a lot of water to help them survive for several days. However, they don't store it in their humps, like many people thought for years. This is an important survival technique, since the animal spends a lot of time in the desert. Camels have other techniques for surviving in the desert, including long eyelashes and small slits in their noses to help protect against dust storms.

MOUNTAIN GOAT

The mountain goat is one of the best climbers in the world of animals. Found in the mountains of the western United States, these cool animals are fun to see, often standing in groups along steep rocks. If you're going on vacation to the mountains, see if these great animals are in that area. Glacier National Park is an especially good area.

LITTLE-KNOWN FACTS

1. Mountain goats have thick fur because they often live in cold areas. They are like the hipsters of the animal world because they have very distinctive beards.
2. Many people know mountain goats as goat-antelopes. This is because they are close relatives to both goats and antelopes.
3. Mountain goats have a cool thing called a cloven hoof. This means they have pads between their hooves that can help them balance on narrow and steep areas.
4. Impressive jumpers, they can leap up to 12 feet!
5. Mountain goats have white fur, which helps them blend in on snowy mountains.
6. Female goats have a fun name. They are called nannies. Males are called billies.
7. Billies often live by themselves. But nannies gather in groups of around twenty, including their young.
8. A group of mountain goats are referred to as a tribe.

Types: One species in North America
Size: 4 to 6 feet
Eats: Grass, moss, other plant matter
Eats Them: Cougars—one of the only predators that can get to them
Range: Parts of the West and up into Alaska

GO OUTSIDE

It's easy to just pay attention to what's in front of you and not around you. But if you do, you might miss out on some pretty cool animals. The next time you're on a hike, make sure to look everywhere, including the tops of trees, the sides of hills and mountains, and around all water areas.

ANIMAL ALL-STAR: Giraffe

The tallest animal in the world deserves a little attention. These beautiful African animals can get up to 18 feet tall, and about half of that is neck. Other things that make this animal unique is its long tongue (up to 18 inches); its large, gorgeous spots; and the fact that both males and females have horns. They are different than other horns, though, because they are mostly made of cartilage instead of bone. Plus, they are covered with skin.

ANIMAL ALL-STAR: Western Gorilla

Out of all the primates in the world, the western gorilla is the largest, reaching up to 6½ feet and more than 400 pounds. Young gorillas spend several months riding on their mother's back or shoulders. Poachers illegally hunt gorillas, and their habitat is being wiped away in many areas, so it's important that we help support efforts to protect them.

BIGHORN SHEEP

Bighorn sheep are a staple sighting of the West. They are especially distinctive because of their enormous curled horns. If you want to see these animals, take a look along rocky bluffs or mountainous areas. They'll often just be hanging out. These are another animal you'll want to put on your list to see. So find out where they're at and plan a trip there.

LITTLE-KNOWN FACTS

1. Relatives of the bighorn sheep include the bison, goat, and antelope.
2. If male bighorn sheep (called rams) have disagreements, they'll often settle them by ramming their horns together. They could do this for hours until one finally gives up and leaves.
3. Bighorn sheep fight for a couple of reasons. First, the males might fight each other for a female. Also, they'll fight to determine the dominant male in a group.
4. They have fantastic balance and can stand on ledges of just 2 inches wide.
5. Both males and females have horns, though the females' will be a little smaller and might not have as much curve to them.
6. The bighorn sheep isn't the only wild sheep in North America. The Dall sheep is another species that you can find in the Northwest.

Types: One species in North America
Size: 5 to 6 feet
Eats: Grasses, sedges, other plants
Eats Them: Mountain lions and other large meat-eaters
Range: Concentrated in the western United States

MUSK OX

Unique animals of the far north, musk oxen haven't changed much in the last 10,000 years. Strong stocky bodies help them survive the harsh climates of the tundra. Musk oxen herds roam together all year long, and they are perhaps most famous for circling up the herd in response to threats. Musk oxen were completely gone from Alaska in the late 1800s, but in the 1930s, thirty-four animals from Greenland were reintroduced to the state. You can still find the species there today.

LITTLE-KNOWN FACTS

1. These animals are actually named for a musky odor that the males release.
2. They know how to stick together. They live in herds year-round.
3. Both males (bulls) and females (cows) sport a unique helmet of horns, and when threatened, the herd circles up and faces their horns outward. You can imagine how this would make predators think twice!
4. Musk oxen have a thing called guard hair. This is what gives them their long, shaggy look, and it can reach up to 2 feet long.
5. The dense fur that keeps musk oxen warm is called qiviut. This is also prized for spinning into wool. Just imagine having some nice and toasty musk ox mittens!
6. During winter, a musk ox can feed on shrubs poking above the snow. It often uses its large hooves like a snow shovel to scrape snow away.
7. Bulls will battle during the rut, or breeding season. It can get dangerous, but their massive horns help protect them from these blows.
8. Young musk oxen begin growing their horns when they are just a month old.
9. Calves can stay with their mothers for 18 months, so the females only breed every other year.

Types: One species
Size: 6 to 9 feet and up to 1,000 pounds
Eats: Grasses, flowering plants, shrubs, mosses, lichens
Eats Them: Wolves, bears, other large meat-eaters
Range: Tundra of the far north

MANATEE

Manatees are gentle giants of the warm waters off the Florida coast. They can sometimes be seen along the Gulf of Mexico and occasionally as far north as Chesapeake Bay and beyond. They will also move into bays, estuaries, rivers, and canals along the coast. Manatees often float just below the water surface, and are sometimes accidentally struck by passing boats.

LITTLE-KNOWN FACTS

1. Dugongs are also in the manatee family. Both of these water creatures are related to elephants. And both have earned the nickname "sea cow."
2. The Steller's sea cow went extinct in the 1700s. Today three species of manatee and one species of dugong remain.
3. Manatees are herbivores, so they mostly eat plant matter.
4. Baby manatees are born in the water.
5. Manatees rarely move faster than a couple of miles per hour, but they can get up to 20 miles per hour.
6. The first laws protecting manatee in Florida were passed in 1893. There are still big conservation efforts today to protect these animals.
7. The lungs of manatees are highly specialized and stretch almost the entire length of the body.
8. Manatees gather at warm-water sources to survive winter's cooler temperatures.

Types: One species in North America
Size: Up to 10 feet and 3,500 pounds
Eats: Mostly aquatic vegetation, especially sea grass
Eats Them: No natural predators
Range: Waters along the Gulf and Atlantic Coasts

WHALE

Whales are some of the most beloved and celebrated creatures of the ocean. Often known for their massive size, whales are fascinating creatures that scientists are still studying and learning more about every year. They can differ a great deal, since there are many whale species in the world. This just makes them even more amazing. You could have an entire book about whales. Actually, there are entire books about whales. But we'll give you a highlight right here.

LITTLE-KNOWN FACTS

1. Many whales feed by just swimming through areas with their mouths open.
2. Gray whales are known for being great migrators. They'll travel more than 10,000 miles each year. This is farther than any other mammal. They usually feed in colder waters and mate and give birth in warmer waters.
3. Have you ever heard of whale "songs"? These are created by humpback whales. This is a form of communication, usually during mating season.
4. Why do we often see whales at the surface? They are mammals after all, so they need to come up to breathe.
5. Young whales (called calves) can stay with their mom for up to a year.
6. All mammals have hair, right? This is true, and whales are no exception. Some whales have little hairs covering their bodies; others have whiskers. So they don't have much, but they do have hair.
7. The killer whale is also known as the orca. They are very popular whales with black and white markings. Orcas eat fish, sharks, whales, and other marine animals.
8. Studies show that whales make friends. Females will be apart for a while, but then they'll come back and float (or hang out) together.

9. The closest relative to a whale is a hippopotamus.
10. Sperm whales are a type of whale that sleeps completely vertical.
11. The largest animal in the world is the blue whale. It can reach more than 100 feet long and weigh 140 tons.
12. Blue whales are extremely loud. They can be heard from more than 100 miles away.
13. Others in the whale family that you might not realize are whales include dolphins and porpoises.
14. The all-white whale, the beluga, continues to be endangered. More conservation efforts are needed to save this amazing creature.

Types: Nearly one hundred species of whale, including dolphins; common North American whales include the blue, killer, and humpback.
Size: A few feet to more than 100 feet
Eats: Plankton, crustaceans, fish, depending on the species
Eats Them: Few predators, though some sharks will attack
Range: Off the coasts of North America

GO OUTSIDE

There's nothing like seeing whales in their natural environment. If you are along the coasts, see if you can sign up for a whale-watching tour. Or if you're taking a ferry or a boat, just look on your own.

DOLPHIN

While dolphins are technically part of the whale family, they still deserve to be separated out and celebrated. They truly are popular and beloved. Dolphin shows at aquariums are one of the main attractions. It's also fun to see if you can catch glimpses of dolphins swimming off the coast if you live along or are visiting the ocean. Movies like *Flipper* (that's an old one) and *Dolphin Tale* have really made these ocean animals soar in popularity.

LITTLE-KNOWN FACTS

1. The tale of a dolphin is called a fluke. Like whales, dolphins have a blowhole at the top of their bodies that they use to breathe.
2. The dorsal fin of dolphins (the fin that sticks up from their bodies) is unique. Take a closer look when you see dolphins, and see if you can notice subtle differences among dorsal fins.
3. Dolphins have a pretty long life for animals. They'll often live fifteen years. Some have even been observed to live for fifty!
4. When dolphins give birth, the babies come out tail first! Those young dolphins might stay with their mom for two or three years before they venture out on their own.
5. Most dolphins are known as saltwater animals, but few species can thrive in freshwater.
6. A group of dolphins is called a pod.
7. Most dolphins have about one hundred teeth. However, they don't use these teeth to chew, since they swallow their prey whole.
8. Dolphins have this cool ability to have only one side of their brain sleep at a time. This way, they are always alert.

Types: Around eight species in North America, including the spinner, white-beaked, and popular bottlenose dolphin
Size: 4 feet to more than 13
Eats: Fish, squid
Eats Them: Sharks, orcas
Range: Off the Atlantic and Pacific coasts of North America

COYOTE

Most animals in the dog family are highly adaptable, and the coyote is no exception. Coyotes are common and thrive throughout North America. Many people fear them because it's not uncommon to see them around backyards and they can look really menacing (especially if you hear stories about how they go after pets). But like most wild animals, they're relatively harmless if you give them their space.

LITTLE-KNOWN FACTS

1. Coyotes can have large litters. While the average number of pups is six, there can be as many as eighteen babies.
2. Like others in the dog family, coyotes use a pouncing technique to catch prey, where they'll jump straight up in the air and then land on their prey.
3. Coyotes can be extremely fast, reaching speeds of 40 miles per hour. This is enough to track down animals as speedy as jackrabbits.
4. They don't hang out in packs quite as much as wolves do, but they will form packs for hunting.
5. Females find a den to have their pups. She'll stay in there with them until their eyes open, which usually takes ten to fifteen days.
6. It's true that coyotes have a bad reputation for eating small dogs. Yes, they will attack small animals, but there's an easy solution to this: Don't leave your small dog outside if you know there are coyotes around.
7. They can smell really well and can even detect prey buried under several feet of snow.

Types: One species in North America
Size: 2 to 4 feet
Eats: Most small animals, like mice and rabbits
Eats Them: Wolves and other larger mammals
Range: Common throughout North America

WOLF

Wolves are part of the dog family, closely related to foxes and coyotes. The gray wolf is the most abundant in North America. These large and fierce animals were once feared by many, but their numbers are much smaller now and they are often celebrated. Wolf conservation efforts are strong throughout the country. Many people are still working to restore this animal and get people to understand it better.

LITTLE-KNOWN FACTS

1. You've probably heard of wolf packs, right? Wolves do travel in packs, which usually include eight to twelve wolves.
2. There's a reason wolves stick together in packs. This way, they are better hunters and can even take down animals like caribou, which can be many times their weight.
3. In the wild dog family, wolves are definitely the largest.
4. Why do wolves howl? They do this as a way to announce themselves and claim territory. They don't, however, howl at the moon. This is a myth, so spread the truth to your friends.
5. Wolves show up often in mythology, Native American stories, and general stories about luck. Perhaps this is why wolves are so celebrated.
6. Gray wolves used to be widespread throughout North America. Today their numbers are greatly reduced. There are concentrated populations near the Rockies, around the Great Lakes, and in Alaska.
7. Red wolves are smaller than gray. They were almost hunted to extinction, but thanks to conservation efforts, they are slowly making a comeback. Still, only one hundred or so live in the wild. This is not a strong number, and more needs to be done to ensure their survival.
8. Some consider the eastern wolf, found around the Great Lakes, a separate species, but it's actually a subspecies of the gray wolf.
9. Wolves do tend to stick together, but sometimes they will drive one away from the pack. When this happens, it's called a lone wolf.

10. Not all animals show affection, but the wolf is an exception. They not only tend to mate for life, but there are examples of them showing affection and defending one another.

Types: Two species in North America—the gray and the red
Size: 3 to 5 feet long
Eats: Small mammals, deer, elk, moose, caribou
Eats Them: Very few except for bears, mountain lions, and people
Range: Northern areas for the gray wolf (which is most widespread) and a small area of North Carolina for the red wolf

GO OUTSIDE

You need your ears for this one. Head out one evening to listen to sounds of the night. Depending on where you are, you could hear coyotes, crickets, and even the haunting howl of wolves. Try to identify at least five different night sounds.

ANIMAL ALL-STAR:
Red Kangaroo

Kangaroos are native to Australia and are well-known animals because of the large pouch the females have in the front. By the way, this pouch will carry an infant kangaroo for as many as 190 days. Kangaroos are also impressive because they can hop on their hind legs at speeds of 30 miles per hour, all while carrying a big tail that can be 2 to 4 feet long!

WILD HORSE

Wild horses! Are these really considered animals of North America? Well, there's actually some controversy around that, since they were introduced here and are not native. They are an icon of the West for many, but they can also damage the rangelands. Lots of people say they still count as a wild animal. And after all, they are wild. These horses are different from the ones that you ride or see on ranches and farms.

LITTLE-KNOWN FACTS

1. Spanish explorers brought wild horses (mustangs) to North America in the sixteenth century.
2. Though the wild horses we know today were introduced here, there are records of real wild horses in North America millions of years ago.
3. Wild horses live in groups, which are led by a female.
4. Scientists are monitoring populations of wild horses. There were more than a million wild horses one hundred years ago, but now they are managed at a population that is less than 25 percent of that number.
5. Perhaps the most famous wild horses in North America are the Chincoteague ponies, which live on an island off the coast of Virginia. Every year they make a famous swim from one island to another, and people gather to watch it.
6. Most of the wild horses in North America now live in Nevada. Check out the Nevada state quarter—you'll see wild horses on it.

Types: The mustang is considered the wild horse of North America.
Size: 5 to 6 feet tall
Eats: Leaves, grass, fruits, other vegetation, some meat
Eats Them: Few natural predators, though some large meat-eating animals will attack wild horses.
Range: Mostly in the West, but also some islands off the Atlantic Coast

PRONGHORN

Pronghorn, sometimes called pronghorn antelopes, are North America's fastest land mammals. With their two large horns, they have a very distinct look. They are not related to the antelopes of Africa and are actually a unique species with no close living relatives. Some migrate long distances between their winter and summer ranges.

LITTLE-KNOWN FACTS

1. Although they look similar to species of antelope in Africa, pronghorn are uniquely North American.
2. Just how fast are they? They can easily reach speeds of more than 50 miles per hour.
3. The horns of pronghorn can be forked, unlike the horns of cows, sheep, and other horned critters.
4. Both males and females have horns, though the female pronghorn grow shorter horns than males. Females also lack the black marking along the throat that males have.
5. Pronghorn live on average about ten years.
6. They have excellent eyesight, which is helpful for living in the wide-open rangelands.
7. The hairs on the rumps of pronghorn actually serve a really good purpose: They can flex these hairs, which alerts others to danger. Yes, it is kind of a butt warning!
8. The Sonoran pronghorn is an endangered subspecies found in Arizona.
9. You might think pronghorn have jumping abilities, but if they came across a fence, they would much rather crawl under it than jump over it.
10. Twins are common for pronghorn.

11. In the early 1900s pronghorn were extremely rare, but they have made a solid comeback in most areas of their range.

Types: One species, found only in North America
Size: 4 to 5 feet
Eats: Grasses, forbs; one of the few species to eat sagebrush
Eats Them: Coyotes, mountain lions, and other large meat-eaters
Range: Western North America from southern Canada to northern Mexico

ANIMAL ALL-STAR:
African Savanna Elephant

Elephants are the largest living land animals, weighing as much as 11 tons. You can find three species total in the world, though the African savanna is the largest. The elephant deserves special recognition because of its trunk, which it uses like a fifth limb. It can lift logs, pull down branches, and squirt water or dust. The end of that trunk also has two edges on it that can curve around, almost like fingers.

MEET THE SMALL MAMMALS

Wait a minute? Didn't we already meet the mammals? To be honest, other than size, there really isn't a difference between a small mammal and a large one. Small mammals have all the features of large mammals. They have hair, most give birth to live young, and females nourish those young with milk. Of course these aren't the only cool mammal features. Let's take another look at mammals to learn more about this popular bunch.

You can't see this when you are just looking at them, but mammals have specialized ear bones that make them unique too. These bones have fun names, such as malleus, incus, and stapes, but sometimes they are referred to as the hammer, anvil, and stirrup because of their shapes.

Mammals have lots of other adaptations and specialized organs that make them mammals, including an area of the brain called the neocortex, which helps regulate many body functions. They also have a four-chambered heart and (with a few exceptions) teeth and a placenta that helps nourish the young before they are born.

Remember that funny word mentioned in the large mammal chapter, referring to animals called monotremes? These animals include echidnas (also known as spiny anteaters) and the somewhat more familiar duck-billed platypus. These mammals are found only in Australia and New Guinea. They all lay eggs, so they are a little different from other mammals.

Kangaroos and their relatives are marsupials. So they are a little different from other mammals too. The opossum is the only marsupial found in the United States and Canada. These mammals give birth to live babies, but they aren't that well developed. The young continue to develop in a pouch until they are more fully grown.

While small mammals have most of the same characteristics as large ones, this is still a large group of animals that include mice, bats, rabbits, squirrels, and chipmunks. Let's learn some more cool facts about this awesome group.

RABBIT

Rabbits are familiar backyard wildlife across much of the country. You might not even think of them as wildlife at first because they are popular pets too. They are probably one of the most common types of wildlife you can find without too much looking. They are also found in diverse habitats, from swamps in the Southeast to the forests of New England to the deserts of the West. You can also see them in parks, woodlots, and farmlands.

LITTLE-KNOWN FACTS

1. Cottontails, the most common rabbits in North America, are named for their short tuft of a tail that resembles a cotton ball.
2. Male rabbits are called bucks; female rabbits are called does. Yep, it's the same names that deer have.
3. Young rabbits are usually born in burrows or thickets, where they stay for a few weeks.
4. You've heard that rabbits are good at hopping, right? Well, they do have good hopping muscles—they can jump more than 8 feet.
5. Rabbits and hares are coprophagic. This fancy word means that they only partially digest their food, so they eat their own poop as a way of getting added nutrients.
6. At only 8 or 9 inches, the pygmy rabbit is the smallest rabbit in North America. They are diggers, and they are found in the sagebrush region of southern Idaho and surrounding states.
7. Rabbits' front teeth never stop growing, but they don't get huge. They are continuously worn down, so they stay at a good size.
8. The eyesight of rabbits is unique. They can see behind their heads but not right in front of their noses.
9. Rabbits also have a unique method for how they sweat: They sweat through the pads of their feet.

10. Are pet rabbits and wild rabbits the same? They look the same, after all. It's definitely not the case, though. Domestic rabbits have a different number of chromosomes than wild rabbits.

Types: A few species in North America, including the eastern cottontail, swamp, and pygmy; many more species around the world
Size: 9 to 20 inches
Eats: Twigs, barks, buds, grasses and forbs
Eats Them: Numerous medium-size predators, including hawks, eagles, owls, bobcats, foxes, and coyotes
Range: Nearly anywhere, from southern Canada across the United States and into Mexico

GO OUTSIDE

Put out a rabbit feast, and see if you can lure them into your backyard. Some of the items you might put out include carrots, lettuce, and any other greens you have on hand. Keep in mind that you might also attract other animals, but be especially on the lookout for rabbits.

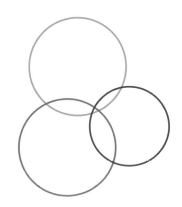

HARE

Hares are closely related to rabbits, but you can still think of them as separate. Hares are the ones from the popular children's story "The Tortoise and the Hare," so they are known for being really speedy. They can be quite fast, but let's take a closer look at this rabbit-like animal to see how they are different.

LITTLE-KNOWN FACTS

1. Some species of hare change colors to match the seasons, although snowshoe hares have white feet all year long.
2. The main difference between rabbits and hares is that hare babies are born fully furred, with open eyes. Baby rabbits, on the other hand, don't have any fur at first, and their eyes are closed. The hares can move around right after birth, but the rabbits have to stay in the nest for a while.
3. Hares tend to make shallow nest depressions aboveground. Like rabbits, hares can have multiple broods of babies every year.
4. Even though they have "rabbit" in their name, jackrabbits are technically a type of hare.
5. So just how fast are hares? Some species can travel up to 45 miles per hour for short bursts.
6. Because of the way they hop, when you see hare and rabbit tracks, the larger tracks (the hind feet) are often in front of their smaller front feet.
7. Hares living in warmer regions (like jackrabbits) have large ears to help keep them cool. Hares living in cold regions (like snowshoe hares) have shorter ears to help prevent frostbite.
8. The arctic hair has a beautiful, pure-white winter coat. In summer it's more of a gray color.
9. There are no true rabbits in Alaska, only hares.
10. Pikas are related to hares and rabbits. They live near the tops of mountains in the West and store vegetation to survive on all winter long.

Types: A handful of species, including the white-tailed and black-tailed jack-rabbits, arctic hare, and snowshoe hare.

Size: Most between 18 and 28 inches

Eats: Grasses, forbs, twigs, barks, buds

Eats Them: Medium-size predators, including weasels, coyotes, lynx, birds of prey, and many others

Range: Jackrabbits are found in the Midwest and West, while hares live in the mountains and parts of Canada and Alaska.

SCIENCE Q&A: How Do You Identify Animal Tracks in the Wild?

When you're out and about or on a hike, you always want to keep an eye on the ground in case you come across cool animal tracks. All species of animals have unique tracks, and you can learn to identify them. Not only is this a cool thing to be able to do, but it can also be useful if you want to know what animals are in the area.

What's the best way to look for tracks? It helps if the tracks are in soft material like snow, mud, or sand. After it rains is also a good time to look for tracks.

How can you tell one track from the next, though? This can be a little tricky. In fact, there are entire books on tracks so you can study the little differences from one track to another. But there are a few things you can look at to help you out, even if you're not experienced at identifying tracks.

You'll want to get a close look. Get right down on the ground with the track, and start studying it. If you are able, take a picture of it so you can compare it later to the tracks in books or online. You can also sketch the track in a book if you like to draw.

Notice how it compares in size to something like your hand or even a dollar bill. How many toes are there? Can you see claw marks in addition to the toes? What else is unique about it?

You should remember that different animals have different prints. For instance, many animals have hooves. And birds have an entirely different track altogether. Once you learn a few basics, it gets a lot easier. But you have to start somewhere, so get out there and start looking for tracks.

WOODCHUCK AND MARMOT

Marmots and woodchucks (also called groundhogs) are closely related. They are the largest of the squirrels in North America. Yes, they really are a type of squirrel. Powerful diggers, these ground squirrels tunnel out extensive holes and burrows. Woodchuck and yellow-bellied marmot are the most widespread species. The next time Groundhog Day comes around, remember that these little guys are also a woodchuck or marmot. Go ahead and test your friends on that fact!

LITTLE-KNOWN FACTS

1. Marmots and woodchucks all hibernate. So only a few are disturbed in an attempt to predict the spring weather. (Psst! Groundhog Day is a fun tradition, but it's more fun than anything else.)
2. They are very good sleepers! Some species can hibernate for nearly ten months.
3. During hibernation, their heart rates can drop to four beats per minutes and they might breathe a single breath every 5 minutes. Now those are some pretty amazing survival techniques.
4. All species have strong front legs and claws that help them dig.
5. The number of names for this animal seems to be never-ending. One nickname for marmots is whistle-pig.
6. The word "woodchuck" might have been derived from a similar-sounding Native American word: "wuchak."
7. Marmots are sometimes called rockchucks because they tend to live in piles of boulders and rocky talus slopes.
8. The Alaska marmot was once considered the same as the hoary marmot, but it is now classified as a separate species.

Types: Six species
Size: 2 to 3 feet and up to 12 pounds
Eats: Grasses and other vegetation
Eats Them: Eagles, wolverines, mountain lions, bears
Range: Woodchucks are found in the East, Midwest, and across Canada. Marmots are found in the western mountains and in pockets of Washington; Vancouver Island, British Columbia; and Alaska.

ANIMAL ALL-STAR: Meerkat

You can't help but love the adorable meerkat, native to South Africa. This little critter, roughly 10 to 12 inches, forms groups of up to thirty or more. They burrow into the ground with their long front claws. They have gained recognition and popularity for the way they stand up on their hind legs. Just watch it for yourself. It's impossible to resist!

CHIPMUNK

You'll recognize chipmunks by the stripes on their faces, but most chipmunk species look about the same. They all have unique chatters, however, and the different species are usually found in different places. Of the more than twenty species in the United States, only the eastern chipmunk is found in the East. The others live from southern deserts to alpine mountaintops in the West.

LITTLE-KNOWN FACTS

1. Chipmunks have cheek pockets inside their mouths. This gives them a storage place for the seeds and nuts they gather up. If you've ever seen a chipmunk with big, bulging cheeks, now you might know why.
2. In warmer areas of the country, chipmunks don't hibernate at all. They can be active all year.
3. Even hibernating chipmunks come out of hibernation throughout the winter and eat seeds they've stored.
4. Young chipmunks leave their parents after two months.
5. Chipmunks can have two litters of three or four babies each year.
6. They can burrow more than 10 feet underground. This is where they will nest, hibernate, and more.
7. California has more than ten species of chipmunks, while states in the East have only one.

Types: More than twenty species
Size: 8 to 10 inches long
Eats: Seeds, nuts, berries, invertebrates, flowers, mushrooms
Eats Them: Weasels, hawks, owls, foxes, others
Range: Found extensively in North America in a variety of habitats

GO OUTSIDE

Chipmunks like peanuts too. So pick up a few peanuts (not the salted ones, like you eat) and put them outside for the chipmunks. It's really fun to watch them come up and take a peanut, one at a time. So when you put them out, don't go too far.

PRAIRIE DOG

Prairie dogs are stout ground squirrels found in the grasslands of western North America. They dig extensive burrow systems and live in large groups called towns. They are considered a keystone species because so many other species depend on the habitats they create.

LITTLE-KNOWN FACTS

1. The scientific name for prairie dogs is *Cynomys*, which is Greek for "mouse dog."
2. Prairie dogs keep the grass trimmed short in their towns. This is one indication that you're in a prairie dog town.
3. In their towns, prairie dogs take turns eating and being on the lookout for predators. This is a really good security method.
4. If danger is detected, prairie dogs let out a sharp barking sound, and everyone scatters for the closest burrows.

5. Don't think these little critters are slow. They can scurry up to 35 miles per hour for short distances.
6. Prairie dogs have special burrows that they use for toilets. Now that's pretty advanced for little critters to have their own toilet system!
7. They have tiny ears that are nearly impossible to see.
8. The largest prairie dogs can weigh up to 4 pounds. That's even bigger than some actual dogs.
9. The endangered black-footed ferret feeds almost exclusively on prairie dogs.
10. Some species of prairie dogs hibernate, while others stay active all winter long.
11. Prairie dogs aren't as widespread as they used to be because of habitat loss and population-control efforts.
12. The national grasslands, Badlands National Park, and Devils Tower National Monument are all great places to watch prairie dogs.

Types: Five species in North America
Size: Most around 15 inches
Eats: Grasses and forbs
Eats Them: Coyotes, badgers, hawks, eagles, rattlesnakes, black-footed ferrets
Range: Western North America, from southern Canada to northern Mexico

ANIMAL ALL-STAR: Capybara

This animal has earned a special title: world's heaviest rodent, reaching up to 4¹/₂ feet and 145 pounds. It looks like a cross between a gopher and a pig. Young capybaras are born with full fur, and after just a few hours, they can run, swim, and dive!

SQUIRREL

Squirrels are one of the most diverse groups of rodents. There are all types, including ground squirrels, tree squirrels, and even flying squirrels. Some squirrels aren't even called squirrels. This is the case with woodchucks and prairie dogs. They are really part of the squirrel family, but you would never know it by their names. Squirrels are common, zipping in and about backyards. They are especially popular (and sometimes greedy) if you have a bird feeder.

LITTLE-KNOWN FACTS

1. Tree squirrels, like gray and fox squirrels, are active year-round, while nearly all ground squirrels hibernate over the winter.
2. Gray and fox squirrels are common in city parks. You can hardly go to a park without seeing a squirrel. Find out what squirrel species are in your area.
3. Not all gray squirrels are gray. They can be much darker, like black or even red.
4. Tree squirrels often live in hollowed-out tree trunks, but they will also build shelters made of leaves.
5. The red squirrel is sometimes called the pine squirrel or chickaree, and it is found in coniferous forests.
6. One sign of red squirrels is a midden, which is pinecone bits that have piled up over the years.
7. Most ground squirrels are pretty plain, but some have spots, lines, or stripes.
8. Antelope squirrels and golden-mantled ground squirrels look like chipmunks, but they don't have stripes on their faces.
9. Flying squirrels don't actually fly; they glide short distances from tree to tree.

10. Squirrel babies are born without their eyes open. They rely on their parents for a few months before they are able to venture out on their own.

Types: Dozens of species
Size: From 8 to 24 inches
Eats: Varies but can include nuts, seeds, berries, mushrooms, insects, eggs, even carrion (dead animals)
Eats Them: Numerous bird and mammal predators
Range: Widespread throughout the United States

GO OUTSIDE

Squirrel nests are actually pretty easy to find. Look up in the trees for a grouping of leaves or twigs together near the base of a branch. It's tempting to think this is a bird's nest at first, but squirrel nests are much bigger. Fall is a good time to see nests once most of the leaves have fallen.

GOPHER

Gophers can be common in an area, but you'll have a hard time seeing one. They spend most of their life underground. With their big feet and powerful legs, they are well suited for this. They have short fur, tiny ears, small eyes, and long, slender bodies. Exclusively vegetarians, gophers feed on plant matter, usually starting at the roots and eating from the bottom up.

LITTLE-KNOWN FACTS

1. Gophers also have a fur lined pouch in their cheeks, and they can turn these inside out.
2. Gophers can completely close their lips behind their front incisor teeth.
3. One of the most visible signs of gophers are tunnel casings left behind.
4. Gophers are active all year and store food in their burrows for winter.
5. Pocket gophers are beneficial by continually churning the soil, although some consider them pests when they are digging in the garden.
6. Much genetics work has been done to distinguish the different species of gophers.
7. Pocket gopher babies are born blind and helpless.
8. Each gopher can move about a ton of soil every year. No wonder people don't like them digging in their gardens.

Types: Approximately thirty-five species
Size: Most 8 to 11 inches
Eats: Vegetation, including roots, stems, leaves, and tubers
Eats Them: Birds, badgers, snakes, lizards
Range: Central and North America; also found in pockets of the United States, excluding the Northeast

SCIENCE Q&A: How Do Animals Survive the Winter?

Winter can be a harsh season to survive. Some species migrate away from the cold in an effort to find food, but not everything is on the move. There are lots of animals that can still thrive in winter, and they'll even use winter to their advantage.

Many species, including jumping mice, some ground squirrels and other rodents, and bears go into varying degrees of torpor or hibernation in winter. They eat extra food in fall. Then their body functions slow down for the winter. They emerge from hibernation in the spring. How is torpor different from hibernation? It's similar but usually not as long.

You can find plenty of species that stay active all winter long. Have you ever seen mouse tracks on top of the snow? Next time, follow them for a bit. Where do they go? Do they seem to disappear at the base of a tree or a shrub, only to reappear somewhere else?

It turns out that snow can make a great blanket for small mammals. They can tunnel and live underneath the snow. This is called the subnivean zone. Lots of times, it is warmer near the ground and under the snow than it is out in the open. If you are a mouse, hiding under the snow is a great way to protect yourself from potential predators like owls and coyotes. It doesn't always work, though, because sometimes predators just plow through the snow after their prey.

Weasels, at least the ones living in the North, have another handy winter adaptation: They turn almost entirely white in winter. But not all weasels change color in winter. Weasels that live in the South stay brown year-round. Other animals change colors for winter survival too.

Another way to survive winter is through food storage. Some animals, like the pika and squirrels, store food that will last them all winter long. Birds will do this too. These food caches are like the kitchen pantry when it's cold.

These are just some of the amazing ways that animals are equipped to handle winter. Let's face it. Winter can be long and cold, but now you know that plenty of animals have what it takes to survive the season.

MOUSE

Mice are found nearly worldwide, and the diversity of species is impressive. Most of these rodents are nocturnal. The vast majority of native North American species thrive in wild areas, but a few will enter human homes, often during winter. Many people fear mice, but when you think about it, unless they get into your house, they don't actually cause any harm, and they're really quite small. If you have a fear of mice, try getting a close look at these little critters. There's nothing to be scared of at all!

LITTLE-KNOWN FACTS

1. There are more than a dozen species of deer mice alone in North America.
2. A mouse heart can beat more than 600 times a minute.
3. Baby mice are born without any hair and are sometimes called pinkies.
4. Harvest mice have grooved upper incisors.
5. The northern pygmy mouse is the smallest rodent in North America, weighing way less than an ounce.
6. Jumping mice have extra-long tails and large hind feet, and, as their name implies, they are excellent jumpers.
7. Only a few species of mice hibernate. Most are active year-round, tunneling along the ground under the snow.
8. Kangaroo rats are really mice related to kangaroo mice and harvest mice. Some might communicate by thumping their large hind feet.
9. Here's another cool fact about kangaroo rats: They have super-efficient kidneys and can survive without drinking water. Instead they get their required moisture from the foods they eat.
10. The house mouse is closely associated with humans. It is found nearly everywhere people are, but it is native to Asia.

Types: More than 1,000 "mouse-like" rodents throughout the world, with several species of mice in North America
Size: Just a few inches for most
Eats: Seeds, grains, fruits, invertebrates
Eats Them: Lots of predators, including snakes, mammals, and birds
Range: You can find mice in every part of North America.

RAT

"Rat" is a term that is applied to a bunch of unrelated animals. North America's native "rats" include woodrats and cotton rats. Both black and brown rats arrived in North American on the ships of early colonists, and they are the rats usually associated with humans and cities. It's true that they aren't very well liked, but they're still part of the animal king-dom, so let's learn about these critters.

LITTLE-KNOWN FACTS

1. Woodrats are sometimes called pack rats for their habit of hoarding objects they collect. This includes both natural and human objects.
2. Woodrats live solitary lives and build extensive stick-pile homes that can reach 8 feet in size.
3. Woodrats have very large eyes, a handy adaptation for these nocturnal animals.
4. Plague, often associated with rats, is a disease that is actually caused by fleas that the rats can host. So even though rats are often associated with disease, they're not always to blame.
5. Cotton rats are so named because they sometimes build their nests out of cotton.

6. Rats can go four days without food. This is a pretty incredible survival technique.
7. In some instances, especially on islands, nonnative rats can cause severe damage to the local ecosystems.
8. You might not know this, but rats are quite the jumpers! They can leap up to 3 feet in the air.
9. Rat teeth can grow up to 4 inches per year, but they are continually worn down by lots of chewing.

Types: Rats are included in the count of mouse-like rodents, more than 1,000 in the world. Most common in the United States is the nonnative brown rat.
Size: 8 to 11 inches for the brown rat
Eats: Scavengers that will eat just about anything, including seeds, grains, fruit, and old food
Eats Them: Coyotes, foxes, snakes, hawks, owls
Range: Rats can be found throughout North America, pretty much everywhere.

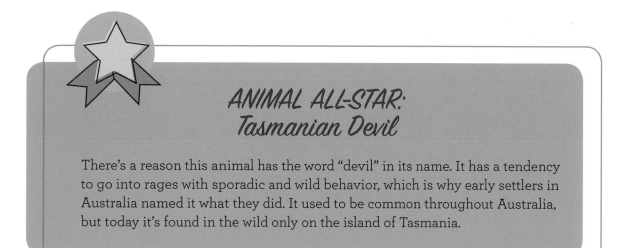

ANIMAL ALL-STAR: Tasmanian Devil

There's a reason this animal has the word "devil" in its name. It has a tendency to go into rages with sporadic and wild behavior, which is why early settlers in Australia named it what they did. It used to be common throughout Australia, but today it's found in the wild only on the island of Tasmania.

MUSKRAT

Muskrats are aquatic rodents. They live in lakes, ponds, slow-moving rivers and streams, and especially marshes. They can be seen swimming along using their skinny tail as a propeller. Another way to know muskrats are in the area is to look for the small lodges they build, often out of cattails or rushes. They will also burrow into streambanks.

LITTLE-KNOWN FACTS

1. Muskrat hind feet are partially webbed to help the animal swim.
2. Despite looking like beavers with skinny tails, they aren't super-close relatives. They are both rodents, though.
3. Muskrats tend to stick together. They live in groups up of to ten.
4. The round-tailed muskrat is found only in Florida and southern Georgia; the common muskrat is found throughout the United States and Canada.
5. The dense muskrat fur traps air. This helps keep them warm and also helps them float.
6. They are great swimmers, and they dive down a lot too. They can stay underwater for up to 15 minutes.
7. As their name implies, muskrats secrete a musky substance, which they use for communication and to mark their territories.
8. Muskrat is a delicacy in some regions of North America, so sometimes hunters will trap them for food and for their fur.
9. Muskrat ears can close so they don't get water in them while they are swimming.
10. Several Native American cultures believe that muskrats have powers. They think that muskrats first brought the land out of the sea.
11. The two muskrat species in the United States are not in the same genus. And neither of them is related to the rats.

Types: Two species in North America
Size: Up to 20 inches
Eats: Mostly aquatic plants
Eats Them: Alligators, mink, coyotes, otters
Range: Widespread in the United States and Canada; also have been released in parts of Europe, Asia, and South America

OTTER

You can't help but admire and adore otters. They are a blast to watch, swimming and diving in and out of the water. You might not think there are otters in your area, but they are pretty widespread, so you might be surprised. Go ahead and check out a river near you for the chance to observe these interesting critters.

LITTLE-KNOWN FACTS

1. Otters inhabit homes along the river, either in a burrow, den, or beaver lodge.
2. Look for otter families in spring. The young are born blind, and their eyes open after about thirty days.
3. They can come on land, but otters are best known for their strong swimming abilities and life in the water. They can swim up to 6 to 7 miles per hour.
4. Even though they can be found in the same areas that you'd find beavers, don't mistake them for one. In fact, otters are more closely related to weasels.
5. Otters have powerful tails that can be up to a foot long. In general, otter tails are about one-third the size of their body.

6. Sea otters are considered to be skilled animals. They have learned how to use tools like rocks, driftwood, or shells to crack open the shells of the prey they eat.

7. While it's only found along a section of the Pacific Coast of North America and Alaska, sea otters deserve a special mention. They grow up to 5 feet. They've suffered in the past because of hunting, but conservation efforts are under way to help protect them for the future.

8. Here's another really cool sea otter fact: They love to eat, and they often do so on their backs! The next time your visit an aquarium, look for the sea otters and watch them eat.

Types: Two species in North America—river otters and sea otters
Size: 25 to 60 inches long
Eats: Snakes, frogs, crayfish, lizards
Eats Them: Coyotes, eagles (river otters); sea lions, sharks (sea otters)
Range: Throughout much of North America except the Southwest for river otter; northern Pacific Coast for sea otter

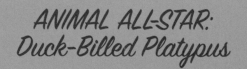

ANIMAL ALL-STAR: Duck-Billed Platypus

These land and water animals of Australia are considered shy, and they do most of their traveling alone. They sure do have a unique look with their webbed feet, duck-like bill, and beaver-like tail. They also have a secret weapon—venom. The male platypus has a spur near its hind foot that delivers venom to its victims.

SHREW

Shrews look like tiny mice with extra-pointy noses. They are some of the smallest mammals in North America, but don't let that fool you. They can also be some of the fiercest. With a super-high metabolism, shrews are always eating. They are active predators that can sometimes kill mice, voles, and other animals even bigger than they are.

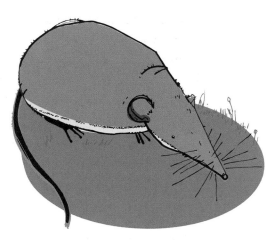

LITTLE-KNOWN FACTS

1. Some shrews have a form of venom that helps them kill their prey.
2. Shrews have dark-colored incisors (front teeth), so it always looks like they need to brush their teeth.
3. The heart rate of a shrew can top 700 beats per minute.
4. Shrews are related to moles.
5. Some species, like elephant, jumping, and tree "shrews," aren't related to the shrews at all. The animal world can sure fool you with names!
6. Shrews have a musk, so very few animals will actually eat them.
7. Some shrews may use echolocation to detect things around them. This is a fancy word for using different sound vibrations and echoes that we can't hear. Dolphins and bats use echolocation as well.
8. Shrews also have a highly developed sense of touch.
9. Water shrews have stiff bristlelike hairs on their feet, allowing them to walk on water for short distances. They are also great swimmers.
10. Water shrews exhale and then quickly inhale when underwater, letting them sniff out their prey.

Types: More than 300 species worldwide
Size: Most about 2 to 4 inches
Eats: Invertebrates and other small prey, which can include mammals and amphibians
Eats Them: Other shrews, mammalian predators, owls, snakes, fish
Range: Shrews are represented by several different species throughout North America.

MOLE

Moles are predators of earthworms, insects, and other invertebrates. Despite looking much like gophers, they aren't related at all. Moles have sausage-shaped bodies, huge front feet for digging, tiny eyes, and no external ears. They are ideal for life underground, although some also actively hunt aboveground and a few underwater.

LITTLE-KNOWN FACTS

1. Moles are related to shrews, and like them have a mild venom to help paralyze their prey. Not a bad trick!
2. Star-nosed moles have super-sensitive fleshy, fingerlike appendages on their faces to help them detect and quickly identify food items.
3. Moles have adaptations that allow them to survive in low oxygen–level conditions.
4. Some, but not all, species form molehills at their burrow entrances.
5. They can dig shallow tunnels up to 12 inches in length per minute.
6. Male moles can be territorial, and their ranges rarely overlap with other males.

Types: More than 400 species of shrews and moles worldwide
Size: Up to 9 inches
Eats: Mostly invertebrates, including worms; some plant material
Eats Them: Hawks, owls, snakes
Range: Numerous species throughout the Northern Hemisphere

BAT

Bats tend to have a bad reputation, but they are seriously cool mammals. A lot of people don't even know they are mammals. In fact, they are the only mammals in the world that can fly! If you've been afraid or cautious of bats in the past, then maybe it's time to give them another chance. There are oodles of interesting facts about them.

LITTLE-KNOWN FACTS

1. There are a lot of myths about bats. The biggest one is that they are blind. There's even that phrase "blind as a bat." This is far from the truth, though. In fact, they actually have really good eyesight.

2. Bats use this cool thing called echolocation. This is when bats send out high-pitched sounds and listen for the sounds to rebound off surrounding objects. Bats detect what's around them and can find their next meal (mostly insects) this way.

3. There are exceptions to what most bats eat. The vampire bat (found mostly in South America but also in parts of Mexico) will bite birds, farm animals, and other mammals and lick their blood for food.

4. Young bats are called pups. And most bats only have one pup a year. This isn't much in the animal world, which is one reason some bat populations are in danger.

5. Bat moms are the coolest. Even if there are hundreds or thousands of other bats around, they can find their young because of their unique smell and sound.

6. Do you know what bat guano is? It's bat poop, and it actually makes really great fertilizer.

7. Look at a picture of a bat skeleton sometime. They are so cool! Their wings are their "hands" and "fingers" that look a lot like yours.

8. Bats are known for gathering in large numbers. Bat colonies can reach into the hundreds or thousands of individual bats.
9. Bats will roost together in caves, roofs, hollow trees, and other areas.
10. Do you live in an area where there are lots of mosquitoes? Put up a bat house. This will help support the bat population, and they'll eat hundreds of mosquitoes every night.
11. Bats can reach speeds of more than 60 miles per hour!
12. Bats can have a really long life—up to thirty years.

Types: More than 1,000 species around the world, with several in North America
Size: Most just a few inches
Eats: Mostly insects, fruit, pollen, nectar
Eats Them: Hawks, weasels, raccoons
Range: Many species found throughout the world

GO OUTSIDE

Go out at dusk, right when it's starting to get dark. Put out a blanket and lie down to watch, because this is when the bats start coming out. As it gets darker, more will come out, swooping and flying around. Many species prefer open areas in the woods or flying over open ponds.

SKUNK

What's the first thing that pops into your mind when you think of a skunk? Is it something along the lines of ewwwww? Yes, these small mammals do have a foul reputation, but if you can look past that, you'll grow to admire these little stinkers.

LITTLE-KNOWN FACTS

1. Not all skunks are striped. Both the eastern and western spotted skunks have a more black-and-white mosaic pattern.
2. Young skunks stay with their mother for up to a year as they learn how to be on their own.
3. When threatened, skunks can omit a horrible odor from under their tail. This is what gives them such a bad reputation. They can shoot this liquid up to 9 feet! The smell can travel half a mile.
4. Some people say that the smelly liquid that a skunk omits is pee, but this is a myth. It sure is a good defense mechanism, though. Skunks have very few predators, which you have to admit is pretty impressive!
5. Skunks can adapt to a wide range of habitats. This includes mountain, prairies, forests, and even backyards. In fact, there are many stories about skunks spraying dogs, so watch out!
6. They are adaptable animals and will go after almost anything for a meal. They even attack beehives because they eat honeybees.
7. They can't see all that well, but they sure do hear and smell great.
8. Skunks live in homes that are usually created by other animals, like dens and burrows. You can also find them living in old logs or empty holes of trees.

Types: Three species in North America—striped, spotted, and hog-nosed
Size: 12 inches for spotted, up to 30 for striped and hog-nosed skunks
Eats: Insects, small mammals, birds, eggs, fish, fruit, seeds
Eats Them: Owls, coyotes, bobcats
Range: Skunks are found throughout North America.

RACCOON

It's not uncommon to see these critters in backyards across North America. They are smart and adaptable animals, learning that humans can lead to a good food source. Sure, they look cute with their black mask across their eyes, but remember they are still wild animals!

LITTLE-KNOWN FACTS

1. Raccoons are scavengers. They will show up in backyards to pick away at food at your bird feeders. They will also go to open garbage cans to find food.

2. These small animals have earned the nickname "masked bandit." They do appear to have a mask across their eyes, but they're like bandits in more than just appearance. They can get into places that most animals can't. They can use their human hand– like paws to open latches and get into areas off-limits to most animals.

3. They might not look very agile, but they can really move. Raccoons can scurry along at nearly 15 miles per hour. They are also great swimmers and climbers.

4. It's a myth that raccoons always wash their food before they eat it.

5. Raccoons can vary a great deal in weight. They can be only 5 or 6 pounds or weigh nearly 60! Part of the reason is that they store up lots of food energy in spring and summer so they can survive through the winter.

6. Raccoons are great climbers. It's not unusual to see them high in a tree, taking a nap.

7. They don't hibernate exactly, but during the winter, raccoons might stay in their dens or holes to sleep for weeks at a time.

Types: One species
Size: Up to 25 inches
Eats: Fruit, plants, frogs, crayfish, mice, eggs
Eats Them: Bobcats, coyotes, owls
Range: Throughout most of North America except far northern regions

ANIMAL ALL-STAR: Red Panda

Is the red panda really a panda? There's been a lot of debate about this over the years, but scientists now agree that it's a cousin to both the giant panda and raccoons. It really belongs in a family all on its own, though. This beautiful animal is native to Asia, and it relies on bamboo leaves for food.

ANIMAL ALL-STAR: Spotted Hyena

Here's a group where the females dominate! Not only are the females slightly bigger than the males, but they are leaders of their group as well. These groups are called clans, and they contain five to fifty hyenas, depending on the habitat. This species is also known as the laughing hyena because it makes a sound that's a lot like a human laugh.

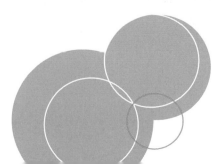

WEASEL

The next time you see tracks in either the mud or snow, take a closer look. You just might see a weasel nearby. These small mammals are located through the northern parts of the United States. Lots of things are related to weasels, including ferrets, minks, badgers, and otters, but there are several species of weasel too. Most people don't realize that they can be fairly common in most areas, but it's true. And who wouldn't want to see a weasel?

LITTLE-KNOWN FACTS

1. Have you ever heard the phrase "that little weasel!"? This can probably be attributed to farmers. Weasels have bad reputations among farmers because they go after their livestock (like chickens). The next time you hear this phrase, you'll know why.
2. They might be small, but weasels have very sharp teeth. They can attack an animal twice their size. No wonder farmers don't want them around their chickens.
3. Like other carnivores (meat-eaters), weasels can't move their jaws from side to side, only up and down.
4. Weasels have white undersides, which many people get the chance to see, since they'll sit upright on their back feet.
5. Some northern species of weasel can change their fur with the seasons. Their fur transforms to white in winter to help them stay hidden. They are active in winter too. This is why you want to keep your eye out for weasel tracks in the snow. White weasels are sometimes called ermine.
6. Weasels in the South don't change colors, even if the same species does change colors in the northern parts of their range.
7. To conserve energy and stay warm, weasels will roll themselves up in a little ball.

Types: Three species in North America—least, short-tailed, and long-tailed
Size: 6 to 10 inches
Eats: Mice, voles, lemmings
Eats Them: Foxes, snakes, birds of prey
Range: Northern parts of North America, Europe, and Asia

BLACK-FOOTED FERRET

Black-footed ferrets are one of the most endangered mammal species in the world. Many people thought they were extinct, but a small population was rediscovered in Wyoming in 1981. Isn't it cool to discover an animal that scientist thought was gone? Since then, conservation efforts have been working to protect and grow the population.

LITTLE-KNOWN FACTS

1. Ferrets are members of the weasel family and are also related to stoats and polecats.
2. It was a cow dog, just doing its job, that discovered the last wild population of black-footed ferrets. The dog was out in the field when it came across one of these "extinct" critters.
3. Captive breeding efforts have led to black-footed ferrets being released in more than twenty locations where they once thrived. This has happened in more than nine states, including Montana, and parts of Canada.
4. Black-footed ferret females are called jills. Males are called hobs. Young ferrets are known as kits.
5. Plague and canine distemper are diseases that have impacted the black-footed ferret recovery efforts.

6. These animals feed almost exclusively on prairie dogs. Young ferrets can kill a prairie dog on their own by the time they are about 90 days old.

Types: Black-footed ferret is the only ferret species in North America.
Size: 18 to 24 inches
Eats: Prairie dogs almost exclusively
Eats Them: Owls, badgers, coyotes
Range: Historically from southern Saskatchewan to northern Mexico

ANIMAL ALL-STAR: Ring-tailed Lemur

It's tempting to lump them in with the monkey family, but lemurs are different. They do spend a lot of time in trees, swinging and jumping from limb to limb, though the ring-tailed lemur tends to spend more time on the ground than other lemurs. Many species are in danger because of habitat loss, and it's important to support efforts to save these big-eyed, long-tailed critters.

ANIMAL ALL-STAR: Warthog

If you take a look at the warthog, chances are you might want to run in the other direction. It looks really scary! Don't worry, though. These African animals are closely related to pigs, and they mostly eat grasses, roots, and plants. They are named for the bumps on their body that look like warts, though they are really there to offer protection.

MINK

If you take one look at a mink, you'll easily see why it's related to the weasel. Both mammals are long and have similar features. In fact, if you saw one in the wild where their geographic ranges overlap, you'd really have to take a closer look to figure out what you're seeing. This is where a field guide can really come in handy. Pick one up and study the small differences between these animals.

LITTLE-KNOWN FACTS

1. Mink have webbed feet, which allow them to hunt both on land and in water.
2. Being able to go easily from water to land is one of the mink's most valuable assets. This means it tries to find a home near the water. This is a major clue if you want to spot a mink. Now you know to look near water.
3. Have you ever heard of a mink coat? Yes, there is a relation between the coat and these little critters. Mink coats are usually made from farm-raised animals.
4. Baby mink are called cubs or kits.
5. The European mink is the other mink in the world, and, yes, it's found in Europe. Very similar to the American mink, it's considered endangered.

Types: One species in North America—the American mink
Size: 1 to 2 feet
Eats: Fish, muskrats, rabbits, frogs
Eats Them: Wolves, foxes, great horned owls
Range: Majority of North America and due to human expansion parts of Europe and Asia

AMERICAN MARTEN

The marten is a small mammal of North America that is closely related to weasels and ferrets. It's also in the same grouping as the fisher, though it's smaller in size. You can find martens in heavily forested areas. Of course you'll have to look up if you want to spot one.

LITTLE-KNOWN FACTS

1. Martens were disappearing in the early 1900s. Conservation efforts have helped restore populations in states like Minnesota.
2. The American marten might also be called pine marten.
3. Martens don't like to share their space. They live alone and are very territorial, so they don't like other martens in their space.
4. They spend most of their time up in trees. They'll even live in trees.
5. The fisher is closely related to the marten. This furry animal's population is even more threatened than the marten.
6. When it snows, martens might burrow underneath several feet of snow for insulation to keep warm.

Types: One species in North America—the American (pine) marten
Size: Around 21 to 30 inches, including the tail
Eats: Mice, chipmunk, squirrels
Eats Them: Fishers, bobcats, hawks, owls
Range: Northern forested areas of the United States and into Canada and Alaska

WOLVERINE

The wolverine is an animal that survives and thrives in cold climates. Don't be fooled by the look of this animal. Sure, it looks like it's related to a bear, but it's actually more closely related to a weasel. It is a short, stocky animal, but it is the largest member of the weasel family. They mostly stick to themselves, making them one of the true loners of the animal world.

LITTLE-KNOWN FACTS

1. The wolverine can cover a lot of ground. In a single day it can travel 15 or 20 miles in search of food. This is quite a ways, considering most animals stick to a very small territory.
2. Not all male animals are bigger than the female, and that's the case here. The male wolverine is only about one-third the size of the female.
3. They have a fantastic sense of smell. For instance, if an animal is burrowed under the snow, a wolverine can smell it 10 to 20 feet deep! This is good for the wolverine, but not so good for that hibernating animal.
4. Wolverines have fascinating paws that are perfect for walking in the snow. When they step down, their foot presses down to nearly twice its size. This means the feet are like snowshoes, built right onto the foot. Try to find a wolverine track or look online to see what one looks like. You'll definitely be surprised.

Types: One species of wolverine in the world
Size: Up to 40 inches
Eats: Rabbits, rodents, caribou, plants and berries in summer, carrion (dead animals)
Eats Them: Larger meat-eating mammals
Range: The northern parts of North America, Europe, and Asia

BADGER

American badgers have very distinct face patterns with white and brown striping (many call it their badge). They are very different from other badgers around the world, and they prefer wide, open areas where they can roam. Badgers have a fierce reputation, known for being aggressive and even mean. So even though it's not that big, don't let the size fool you.

LITTLE-KNOWN FACTS

1. Badgers are amazing excavators. They have long claws that are designed to dig. Then their feet in the back are almost like little shovels, pushing the dirt through and helping to create a safe haven.

2. All this digging is helpful. Badgers can both hear and smell really well. They dig in an area where there are rodents, and soon they'll have their next meal.

3. Move over skunks! If badgers are threatened, they can also release a foul odor that warns their predators to get away.

4. It's not easy for predators to get badgers. First of all, they are very vocal and will hiss and growl to scare attackers off. Next, they have a thick and muscular neck area, so predators will have a hard time carrying one off in their mouth. So they might attack a badger, discover they can't carry it, and then leave it be.

5. You might not know it by looking, but badgers have very powerful jaws. In fact, they have thirty-four teeth, including four very sharp canines.

Types: One species, American badger, in North America
Size: Up to 28 inches
Eats: Small mammals like prairie dogs, ground squirrels
Eats Them: Coyotes and other large mammals
Range: Much of the western half of the United States

ARMADILLO

The armadillo carries its own suit of armor: a hard shell that helps protect it from predators. It has some of the most natural protection around. This is good, since it doesn't move all that fast, even if a predator is after it. Most armadillos are found in South America, though there is one species you can look for when you're visiting the southern United States.

LITTLE-KNOWN FACTS

1. The middle of this armadillo species has bony bands in the center—hence the name nine-banded armadillo. In reality, they have eight to ten bands. So what's with the bands? They allow the animal to be flexible, which can come in handy when moving around or escaping predators.

2. The armor and bony skin of this animal accounts for about one-sixth of its overall weight, which can be up to 14 pounds.

3. Here's something unique about the offspring: This species of armadillo nearly always have quadruplets, which is four babies, and they're all the same sex.

4. All armadillos are diggers and can dig out an impressive burrow to live. Their short, powerful arms are designed to help dig. Many other animals appreciate their digging too. Rabbits, burrowing owls, and other animals will use their abandoned burrows.

5. Many people think of armadillos rolling up in a ball to defend themselves. This is true, but only for two species of armadillos, neither of which is found in North America.

Types: One species, the nine-banded armadillo, in North America
Size: Up to 22 inches
Eats: Ants, birds, fruit, roots
Eats Them: Coyotes, cougars, wolves, bears
Range: Southern United States

BOBCAT

If you were to look at the face of a bobcat, you'd swear you were looking at a short-haired cat that you might see at someone's house. They do have some pretty similar catlike habits, though. Of course this doesn't make them a friendly cat, so it's best to stay away. Most animals are more afraid of you than you are of them. But if they have young nearby, they can be aggressive.

LITTLE-KNOWN FACTS

1. Bobcats are named for their short tails, which look like they have been bobbed (cut short). Their tails are only 4 to 7 inches long.
2. Also referred to as wildcats, bobcats are about twice the size of domestic kitties.
3. Bobcats are seldom seen. They are nocturnal, so that's one reason, but they are also stealthy, elusive travelers.
4. Like domestic cats, young bobcats are called kittens. They stay with their mother for six to nine months, learning how to hunt and survive, before they go out on their own.
5. Also similar to domestic cats, bobcats are excellent pouncers. They can leap up to 10 feet in the air, which helps them attack their prey.
6. The lynx, the closest relative to bobcats, lives in snowy regions.

Types: One species in North America
Size: From 26 to 44 inches
Eats: Rabbits, hares, rodents, deer
Eats Them: Larger meat-eaters, like mountain lions
Range: Throughout Mexico, southern Canada, and much of the United States

FOX

Foxes have a reputation for being stealthy—they can come and go without you even knowing they're around. You can find five total fox species in North America, though the red fox is the most common and widespread. These small, doglike animals wander both cities and rural areas. Since they mostly hunt at night, it makes them even harder to see. If you do want to see one, you should especially keep an eye out around dusk.

LITTLE-KNOWN FACTS

1. Foxes are members of the dog family, along with wolves and coyotes. They're all considered canids.
2. While some members of the canids (like wolves) live in groups called packs, foxes usually live alone.
3. Female foxes are called vixens.
4. Young foxes are called kits or cubs. When they're little, they have to watch out for eagles, which might swoop down to get them.
5. The gray fox, also fairly common in North America, has unique claws and can climb trees almost like a cat!
6. Foxes make a lot of different noises—one sounds like a cross between a dog bark and a parrot squawk.
7. Foxes are among the group of mammals that use burrows. Though they can have homes aboveground, they prefer find one underground.

Types: Five species in North America—red, kit, swift, arctic, and gray
Size: Most are 23 to 30 inches. Swift and kit foxes can be as small as 13 inches.
Eats: Rabbits, mice, beetles, worms, frogs, birds, fruit
Eats Them: Coyotes, wolves, bears, mountain lions
Range: Red and gray foxes are found throughout the lower forty-eight states. Kit and swift foxes are found only in small areas in the western and central United States. Arctic fox habitat is in northern Canada and Alaska.

GO OUTSIDE

Search for a den that looks like a fox could use it. Don't go digging around in it, but use this opportunity to think like a fox. What would make a good home? Where would you go at night? Once you start thinking like an animal, you just might see a few along the way.

OPOSSUM

You might think opossums lack that cute cuddly look. Yes, they do look a bit scraggly, and they have a tail that looks more like a rat's tail than anything else. They are pretty fascinating nocturnal animals, though. If you come across an opossum, chances are, you're going to think it's dead. Don't let it fool you!

LITTLE-KNOWN FACTS

1. Opossums are in the marsupial family—the same group as kangaroos!
2. If they're threatened, opossums will pretend to be dead, hoping the predator will go away. They can stay curled up this way for several hours. This is where the phrase "playing possum" came from.
3. You can find one main species of opossum in North America—the Virginia opossum.
4. They have very impressive tails, which can be longer than their bodies at 10 to 22 inches.
5. Opossums have fifty teeth. They'll use these teeth to stop by a backyard and nibble on dog food, bird seed, or garbage.
6. When an opossum baby is born, it's about the size of a dime! They have a lot of growing to do before they can be on their own. Following birth, they live in a pouch (similar to a kangaroo pouch) for two to three months.

7. Many people think opossums carry rabies, but actually this is extremely rare.
8. Contrary to a popular myth, the opossums of North America don't sleep hanging upside-down by their tails.

Types: One species, Virginia opossum, in North America
Size: 13 to 20 inches
Eats: Eggs, frogs, insects, fruit
Eats Them: Mountain lions, wolves, bears, other large predators
Range: Central and southeastern part of the United States, Mexico, and along the West Coast

GO OUTSIDE

Everyone should see an opossum "playing possum" at least once. Now you shouldn't approach an opossum if you see it on the ground. Always give it space. But it's a good nature goal to see this survival technique for yourself.

ANIMAL ALL-STAR: Koala

Native to eastern Australia, the koala spends all of its life in eucalyptus trees, where the leaves make up almost its entire diet. Some people have called this climber a bear and many still call it a koala bear, but it is not in the bear family at all. Though its thick body and face are very bearlike, don't be tempted to classify it as one. Like kangaroos, koalas are in the marsupial family, so the mothers will carry the young in its pouch for nearly six months.

BEAVER

If you think you see a beaver, then you must be near the water.
These critters have webbed feet, which are great for swimming.
In general, water is a big part of their lives. They build their
homes on lakes, ponds, and slow-moving rivers and streams,
giving them some added protection from predators. So the next time you see a big pile of logs
and sticks out in the water, take a second
glance for a furry critter sticking up among
the mess.

LITTLE-KNOWN FACTS

1. Beavers are part of the rodent group.
   They have large incisors, which they use
   for gnawing on wood.
2. These animals have a really cool third eyelid
   that is transparent. It comes down over the eye when they're swimming,
   so they can see underwater.
3. Beavers are smart in building their homes on water. For added
   protection, they make the entrance only accessible under the water, so it
   really keeps predators away.
4. Young beavers often stay with their parents for a couple of years. If you
   see one beaver, there's a good chance you'll see up to five more.
5. Beavers have huge, flat tails that can be a foot long or more. So what
   do they do with these tails? Primarily, they're used to slap the water,
   warning other beavers in the area of potential danger.

Types: One species, American beaver, in North America
Size: 30 to 35 inches
Eats: Leaves, twigs, bark, water plants
Eats Them: Foxes, coyotes, wolves, weasels, eagles, owls
Range: Most of North America except for the Southwest and Mexico

GO OUTSIDE

Find signs of a beaver. This can include a gnawed up tree alongside the river or a group of branches and twigs damming off part of the water. It's not hard to find once you know what to look for. Then you'll know where to go if you want to spot a beaver.

SCIENCE Q&A: What Is a Keystone Species?

Nature is all connected. Everything affects everything else. But some animals have major impacts on the rest of nature, and these are known as keystone species. Like the top rock in a stone arch, they support a whole range of other critters. Keystone species can change the surrounding areas, and other species can be dependent on these changes.

Let's take a look at a specific animal example. Beavers are considered a keystone species. One reason is because they gnaw down trees. They also build dams that block up flowing water. Beaver dams can create a whole pond by damming up a section of river or stream. This is a big change to the landscape. Beaver pond areas can provide habitat for a wide range of species. Fish and amphibians will take advantage of these waters. So will birds and mammals. The plants will also change because of the beavers. See how their behavior is affecting many others?

Prairie dogs are another classic keystone species. Prairie dogs live in large colonies, and they dig extensive burrows in the prairies. But prairie dogs aren't the only animals that use these burrows. How many animals can you think of that live in prairie dog towns? There can be dozens of other species living in these burrows—things as diverse as badgers and burrowing owl to rattlesnakes and bison. Even spiders and toads will use these burrows. So, again, you can see how prairies dogs change the landscape, and how other animals are dependent on these changes.

While everything in nature affects everything else, the species that change things in a way that benefits other animals are the keystones.

PORCUPINE

Just take one look at a porcupine and you can easily tell that it's sending a "stay away" message. The quills that cover its body offer amazing protection from other animals. If you have a curious dog, make sure it doesn't come face to face with this prickly animal—your pet will be sorry it did.

LITTLE-KNOWN FACTS

1. Porcupines are actually a large rodent. True, you probably think of mice or rats when you think of rodents, but now you can add porcupines to that list as well.
2. Though you can't see it very well, under all those quills, porcupines are covered in fur.
3. If porcupines lose their quills—either from puncturing something or just falling out—they will grow new ones.
4. Those quills are pretty small, and they really add up. Overall, one porcupine can have 20,000 to 30,000 quills!
5. When baby porcupines (called porcupettes) are born, they have soft quills. The quills harden after a few days.
6. It's true that most animals leave porcupine alone, but it does have a few predators. How do those predators eat them? They flip porcupines over, because there aren't quills on the stomach.
7. There's a rumor that porcupine can shoot their quills. This isn't true, but you still don't want to have a run-in with these animals.
8. A group of porcupines is called a prickle.

Types: One species, North American porcupine, on this continent
Size: 26 to 32 inches
Eats: Bark, twigs, nuts, other plants
Eats Them: Bobcats, cougars, fishers
Range: Throughout the top half of North America

GO OUTSIDE

Here's another item to look for outside, though this one is small and tricky. Try to find porcupine quills in nature. If you think it's like searching for a needle in a haystack, you're right. Quills are needlelike, and they can be extremely hard to spot on the ground. Still, it's a fun thing to look for when you're out on a hike.

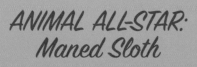

ANIMAL ALL-STAR:
Maned Sloth

Think a sloth is a type of monkey? Think again! Sloths might seem like tree-swinging monkeys, but they are actually more closely related to anteaters. They are considered arboreal. This just means they spend nearly all their lives up in trees. The maned sloth is found in South America, and like its other sloth cousins, it's a great swimmer when it comes down from the trees.

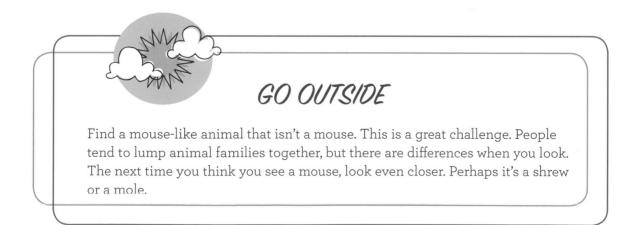

GO OUTSIDE

Find a mouse-like animal that isn't a mouse. This is a great challenge. People tend to lump animal families together, but there are differences when you look. The next time you think you see a mouse, look even closer. Perhaps it's a shrew or a mole.

JAVELINA

The javelina has lots of names, including peccary and skunk pig. This little critter is closely related to the pig family, but try not to think of it as a pig. It's really its own animal. When you see them, it might be tempting to classify them as a pet, because they do resemble those pot-bellied pigs that some people have as pets. But just remember that they are wild animals.

LITTLE-KNOWN FACTS

1. There's a reason javelinas have earned the nickname "skunk pig." They have a scent gland on top of their rump, which they rub on objects to mark their territory. By the way, this scent doesn't exactly smell great to many.
2. Javelinas stick together. They might form a group of fifty or more.
3. Young javelinas can be called reds because of the reddish color of their hair.
4. They are mostly active at night.
5. To cool off, they will roll around in the mud.

Types: One species in North America
Size: 30 to 40 inches
Eats: Mostly plant material, including roots, bulbs, and berries; also worms, grubs, lizards
Eats Them: Mountain lions, coyotes, bobcats
Range: Southwest United States and into Mexico and South America

ANIMALS BY STATE AND PROVINCE

It's common for states to designate an official state bird, but it doesn't end there. Many states and Canadian provinces have official mammals, reptiles, butterflies, and even fish. Here's a look at each state and province, highlighting the official animals for each one.

United States

ALASKA
Bird: Willow ptarmigan
Fish: King salmon
Insect: Four-spot skimmer dragonfly
Land mammal: Moose
Marine mammal: Bowhead whale

HAWAII
Bird: Nene (Hawaiian goose)
Fish: Humuhumunukumukuapua'a
Insect: Kamehameha butterfly
Mammal: Hawaiian monk seal
Marine mammal: Humpback whale

WASHINGTON
Amphibian: Pacific chorus frog
Bird: American goldfinch
Fish: Steelhead trout
Insect: Green darner dragonfly
Mammal: Olympic marmot
Marine mammal: Orca whale

OREGON
Animal: American Beaver
Bird: Western meadowlark
Fish: Chinook salmon
Insect: Oregon swallowtail butterfly

CALIFORNIA
Animal: California grizzly bear
Bird: California quail
Fish: California golden trout
Insect: California dogface butterfly
Marine fish: Garibaldi
Marine mammal: California gray whale
Reptile: Desert tortoise

MONTANA
Animal: Grizzly bear
Bird: Western meadowlark
Butterfly: Mourning cloak
Fish: Blackspotted cutthroat trout

IDAHO
Bird: Mountain bluebird
Fish: Cutthroat trout
Insect: Monarch butterfly
Raptor: Peregrine falcon

nevada

utah colorado

arizona

new mexico

WYOMING
Bird: Western meadowlark
Fish: Cutthroat trout
Mammal: Buffalo (Bison)
Reptile: Horned lizard

NORTH DAKOTA
Bird: Western meadowlark
Fish: Northern pike

SOUTH DAKOTA
Animal: Coyote
Bird: Ring-necked pheasant
Fish: Walleye
Insect: Honeybee

NEVADA
Animal: Desert bighorn sheep
Bird: Mountain bluebird
Fish: Lahontan cutthroat trout
Reptile: Desert tortoise

UTAH
Animal: Rocky Mountain elk
Bird: California gull
Fish: Bonneville cutthroat trout
Insect: Honeybee

COLORADO
Animal: Rocky Mountain bighorn
   sheep
Bird: Lark bunting
Fish: Greenback cutthroat trout
Insect: Colorado hairstreak butterfly
Reptile: Western painted turtle

ARIZONA

Amphibian: Arizona tree frog
Bird: Cactus wren
Butterfly: Two-tailed swallowtail
Fish: Apache trout
Mammal: Ringtail
Reptile: Arizona ridge-nosed
    rattlesnake

NEW MEXICO

Amphibian: New Mexico spadefoot
    toad
Animal: Black bear
Bird: Greater roadrunner
Butterfly: Sandia hairstreak butterfly
Fish: New Mexico cutthroat trout
Insect: Tarantula hawk wasp
Reptile: New Mexico whiptail lizard

NEBRASKA

Bird: Western meadowlark
Fish: Channel catfish
Insect: Honeybee
Mammal: White-tailed deer

KANSAS
Amphibian: Barred tiger salamander
Animal: Buffalo (Bison)
Bird: Western meadowlark
Insect: Honeybee
Reptile: Ornate box turtle

MISSOURI
Amphibian: North American bullfrog
Animal: Missouri mule
Aquatic animal: Paddlefish
Bird: Eastern bluebird
Fish: Channel catfish
Insect: Honeybee
Invertebrate: Crayfish
Reptile: Three-toed box turtle

OKLAHOMA
Amphibian: Bullfrog
Animal: Buffalo
Bird: Scissor-tailed flycatcher
Butterfly: Black swallowtail
Fish: White bass
Flying mammal: Mexican free-tailed bat
Fur-bearing animal: Raccoon
Insect: Honeybee
Reptile: Collared lizard

ARKANSAS
Bird: Northern mockingbird
Butterfly: Diana fritillary
Insect: Honeybee
Mammal: White-tailed deer

TEXAS
Bird: Northern mockingbird
Fish: Guadalupe bass
Flying mammal: Mexican free-tailed bat
Insect: Monarch butterfly
Large mammal: Texas longhorn
Reptile: Texas horned lizard
Small mammal: Nine-banded armadillo

MINNESOTA
Bird: Common loon
Butterfly: Monarch
Fish: Walleye
Reptile: Blanding's turtle

IOWA
Bird: American goldfinch

WISCONSIN
Animal: Badger
Bird: American robin
Fish: Muskie
Insect: Honeybee
Wildlife animal: White-tailed deer

ILLINOIS
Amphibian: Eastern tiger salamander
Animal: White-tailed deer
Bird: Northern cardinal
Fish: Bluegill
Insect: Monarch butterfly
Reptile: Painted turtle

INDIANA

Bird: Northern cardinal

MICHIGAN

Bird: American robin
Fish: Brook trout
Mammal: White-tailed deer
Reptile: Painted turtle

OHIO

Animal: White-tailed deer
Bird: Northern cardinal
Insect: Ladybug
Reptile: Black racer snake

PENNSYLVANIA

Animal: White-tailed deer
Bird: Ruffed grouse
Fish: Brook trout
Insect: Firefly

MARYLAND

Bird: Baltimore oriole
Crustacean: Blue crab
Fish: Striped bass
Insect: Baltimore checkerspot
    butterfly
Reptile: Diamondback terrapin turtle

DELAWARE
Animal: Horseshoe crab
Bird: Blue hen chicken
Bug: Ladybug
Butterfly: Tiger swallowtail
Fish: Weakfish
Macro-invertebrate: Stonefly
Wildlife animal: Gray fox

NEW JERSEY
Animal: Horse
Bird: American goldfinch
Bug: Honeybee

NEW YORK
Animal: American Beaver
Bird: Eastern bluebird
Freshwater fish: Brook trout

Insect: Nine-spotted ladybug
Reptile: Snapping turtle
Saltwater fish: Striped bass

MAINE
Animal: Moose
Bird: Black-capped chickadee
Fish: Landlocked salmon
Insect: Honeybee

VERMONT
Amphibian: Northern leopard frog
Bird: Hermit thrush
Butterfly: Monarch
Cold-water fish: Brook trout
Insect: Honeybee
Reptile: Painted turtle
Warm-water fish: Walleye

CONNECTICUT
Animal: Sperm whale
Bird: American robin
Insect: European praying mantis
Fish: American shad
Shellfish: Eastern oyster

RHODE ISLAND
Bird: Rhode Island red (chicken)
Fish: Striped bass

VIRGINIA
Bat: Virginia big-eared bat
Bird: Northern cardinal
Fish: Brook trout
Insect: Tiger swallowtail

WEST VIRGINIA
Animal: Black bear
Bird: Northern cardinal
Butterfly: Monarch
Fish: Brook trout
Insect: Honeybee
Reptile: Timber rattlesnake

KENTUCKY
Animal: Gray squirrel
Bird: Northern cardinal
Butterfly: Viceroy
Insect: Honeybee

TENNESSEE
Amphibian: Tennessee cave
    salamander
Bird: Northern mockingbird

NEW HAMPSHIRE
Amphibian: Spotted newt
Animal: White-tailed deer
Bird: Purple finch
Butterfly: Karner blue
Freshwater fish: Brook trout
Game fish: Striped bass
Insect: Ladybug

MASSACHUSETTS
Bird: Black-capped chickadee
Fish: Cod
Insect: Ladybug
Mammal: Right whale
Reptile: Garter snake

Butterfly: Zebra swallowtail
Commercial fish: Channel catfish
Insect: Firefly, ladybug, and honeybee
Reptile: Eastern box turtle
Sport fish: Smallmouth bass
Wild animal: Raccoon

NORTH CAROLINA
Bird: Northern cardinal
Fish: Channel bass
Freshwater fish: Southern
  Appalachian brook trout
Insect: Honeybee
Mammal: Gray squirrel
Reptile: Eastern box turtle

SOUTH CAROLINA
Amphibian: Spotted salamander
Animal: White-tailed deer
Bird: Carolina wren
Butterfly: Tiger swallowtail
Fish: Striped bass
Insect: Carolina mantid
Reptile: Loggerhead sea turtle
Spider: Carolina wolf spider

LOUISIANA
Amphibian: Green tree frog
Bird: Brown pelican
Crustacean: Crawfish (Crayfish)
Freshwater fish: White perch
Insect: Honeybee
Mammal: Louisiana black bear
Reptile: American alligator
Saltwater fish: Spotted seatrout

MISSISSIPPI
Bird: Northern mockingbird
Butterfly: Spicebush swallowtail
Fish: Largemouth bass
Insect: Honeybee
Land mammal: Red fox and
  white-tailed deer
Marine mammal: Bottlenose dolphin
Reptile: American alligator
Waterfowl: Wood duck

ALABAMA

Amphibian: Red hills salamander
Bird: Northern flicker
Butterfly: Eastern tiger swallowtail
Freshwater fish: Largemouth bass
Insect: Monarch butterfly
Mammal: Black bear
Marine mammal: West Indian
  manatee
Reptile: Alabama red-bellied turtle
Saltwater fish: Fighting tarpon

GEORGIA

Amphibian: Green tree frog
Bird: Brown thrasher
Butterfly: Tiger swallowtail
Fish: Largemouth bass
Insect: Honeybee
Mammal: Right whale
Reptile: Gopher tortoise

FLORIDA

Animal: Florida panther
Bird: Northern mockingbird
Butterfly: Zebra longwing
Fish: Largemouth bass
Marine mammal: Manatee
Reptile: American alligator
Saltwater mammal: Dolphin
Saltwater reptile: Loggerhead sea
  turtle
Tortoise: Gopher tortoise

Canada

YUKON
Bird: Common raven

NORTHWEST TERRITORIES
Bird: Gyrfalcon

NUNAVUT
Bird: Rock ptarmigan

BRITISH COLUMBIA
Animal: Spirit bear
Bird: Steller's jay
Fish: Pacific salmon

ALBERTA
Animal: Bighorn sheep
Bird: Great horned owl
Fish: Bull trout

SASKATCHEWAN
Animal: White-tailed deer
Bird: Sharp-tailed grouse
Fish: Walleye

MANITOBA
Animal: Plains bison
Bird: Great gray owl
Fish: Walleye

ONTARIO
Bird: Common loon

QUEBEC
Bird: Snowy owl

NEW BRUNSWICK
Bird: Black-capped chickadee

LABRADOR
Bird: Atlantic puffin

NEWFOUNDLAND
Animal: Caribou
Bird: Atlantic puffin

NEW BRUNSWICK
Bird: Black-capped chickadee

NOVA SCOTIA
Bird: Osprey

PRINCE EDWARD ISLAND
Bird: Blue jay

INDEX

ABOUT THE AUTHORS

Stacy Tornio is a master gardener, master naturalist, and the author of six books, all dedicated to getting kids and families outside. Though she's a native Oklahoman, she now resides in Milwaukee, where she enjoys watching her two children explore nature in their own backyard and beyond. Stacy loves gardening and even had her own veggie stand at the farmer's market when she was a kid. Today, she's still growing veggies, along with lots of other plants and flowers. She enjoys trying unique varieties like purple carrots, orange coneflowers, and any type of daisy. Stacy also worked on the national birding and gardening magazine, *Birds & Blooms*, for ten years.

Ken Keffer was born and raised in Wyoming. A naturalist and environmental educator, he has worked in Alaska, Maryland, New Mexico, Ohio, Wisconsin, and the Gobi Desert of Mongolia. During this time, he's studied flying squirrels, camels, prairie dogs, and lots and lots of birds. Ken is a freelance writer—you can see his articles regularly in *Birds & Blooms*, *Outdoors Unlimited*, and *Parks and Recreation* magazines. When he's not traveling or educating others about nature, he enjoys birding, snowshoeing, fly fishing, and walking his dog, Willow the Wonder Mutt.

Visit Stacy and Ken's website, destinationnature.net, to learn more about them and their books.

ken and stacy